FIELD, COVER, AND TRAP SHOOTING

FIELD, COVER, AND TRAP SHOOTING

Adam H. Bogardus

A General Books LLC Publication.

Modifications Copyright ©2009 by General Books LLC. All rights reserved.

Published by General Books LLC.

You may not reproduce this book, stored it in a retrieval system, or transmitted in any form or by any means, electronic, mechanical, photocopying, recording, scanning, or otherwise, except as permitted under Section 107 or 108 of the 1976 United States Copyright Act, without either the prior written permission of the Publisher, or authorization through payment of the appropriate per-copy fee to the Copyright Clearance Center, Inc., 222 Rosewood Drive, Danvers, MA 01923, (978) 750-8400, fax (978) 646-8600, or on the web at www.copyright.com.

Limit of Liability/Disclaimer of Warranty: While the publisher and author have used their best efforts in preparing this book, they make no representations or warranties with respect to the accuracy or completeness of the contents of this book and specifically disclaim any implied warranties of merchantability or fitness for a particular purpose. No warranty may be created ore extended by sales representatives or written sales materials. The advice and strategies contained herin may not be suitable for your situation. You should consult with a professional where appropriate. Neither the publisher nor author shall be liable for any loss of profit or any other commercial damages, including but not limited to special, incidental, consequential, or other damages. Please keep in mind that this book was written long ago; the information in it is not current.

We have recreated this book from the original using Optical Character Recognition software to keep the cost of the book as low as possible. Therefore, could you please forgive any spelling mistakes, missing or extraneous characters that may have resulted from smudged or worn pages? When in doubt, please consult the original scanned book which may be available from our website.

For information on our books please go to www.general-books.net.

CONTENTS

1	Section 1	1
2	Section 2	9
3	Section 3	17
4	Section 4	23
5	Section 5	29
6	Section 6	41
7	Section 7	47
8	Section 8	53
9	Section 9	61
10	Section 10	67
11	Section 11	73
12	Section 12	79
13	Section 13	93
14	Section 14	97
15	Section 15	113

16 Section 16 117

1

SECTION 1

Field, Cover, And Trap Shooting.
   CHAPTER I.
   GENERAL INTRODUCTORY REMARKS.
   Within a comparatively recent period the numbers of those who follow the delightful and healthful sports of the field have increased almost beyond calculation in this country, and they are still rapidly augmenting. Among all those sports there is none so easy of attainment, and certainly none so invigorating, useful, and enjoyable, as the pursuit of game-birds, waterfowl, etc., over dogs, or, at flight time, in the neighborhood of the haunts of the latter. The vast extent and variety of our territory|woodland interspersed among prairie, pasture, and cultivated farms|the great abundance of game to be met with by those who know when and where to seek for it, and the many kinds to be found in these favorite haunts at the proper seasons, afford such excellent and varied shooting as may hardly be experienced if sought for anywhere else. The art of shooting swift-flying birds on the wing is of comparatively recent origin in this country. Years ago but few people followed it, and they had mostly acquired their skill in Europe before they came here. The quickness and art necessary for even moderate success were almost comparatively unknown in the regions where such game most abounded, and they were in a great measure deemed worthless, of no more practical

use than the curious tricks of a juggler. This was not unnatural. The backwoodsmen, and those settlers who had made lodgments in the immense prairies of the Western States, could kill a buck with the rifle, or knock over a fat turkey with the same arm ; and those who had old-fashioned smoothbores seldom shot with anything less than buckshot, or the largest sizes of other shot. Hence they looked with a sort of lazy curiosity akin to contempt upon the doings of the men who, with good guns and small shot, killed " little birds," as quail, plover, woodcock, snipe, etc., were denominated. The use of the setter and pointer was practically unknown. The game was considered to be a trifling matter, not worth the powder and shot expended upon it. The latter were somewhat dear, and money was very scarce. The huntersand Indians called the shot-gun by the derisive term " squaw gun," and wondered that grown men should delight in its use. All that is now greatly changed. Thousands every year enjoy sport of the highest order, and fill their bags in the most artistic manner, in many parts of the country where shooting on the wing was formerly unknown. Shooting of this sort once enjoyed is never willingly relinquished altogether. Those who are able to afford the cost and spare the time from their avocations in the great cities impatiently count the days which must intervene before the time comes for them to jump aboard the train with their guns and their sporting paraphernalia, bound to the shooting-grounds|the places where game is to be found in abundance. Arrived in these sections, and meeting with old friends, the harassed and weak grow vigorous again, and the strong become stronger. The consciousness of skill, the confidence begotten of success, give such a spring to the mind and nerves, and inflame the ardor of pursuit to such a degree, that the fatigues of the excursion are scarcely perceived, and ita privations, if such they may be called, are laughed at and merrily endured till speedily forgotten. The habits of the various kinds of game are a subject of great interest and observation. The fine andeager instinct of the dogs, their great sagacity, endurance, and patience, are remarked with pride and admiration. The features of the varied landscapes |hill and vale, woodland and riverside, vast prairies with groves and fringes of timber on the branches of winding and meandering streams, broad fields of land, now in pasture, now covered with brown stubble, now waved over by the green flags of the corn, tall, strong, and a place of refuge for quail, grouse, etc.|afford constant pleasure to the sportsman. And after the labors and sports of the day are done, the camp-fire beneath the trees, on the banks of a stream, or the margin of a little lake, is a place of calm recreation and repose. You may hear the call of the night-birds, and the low, suppressed noises of the nocturnal animals afoot after their prey, but neither the hoot of the owl nor the howl of the wolf will drive slumber from the pillow of brush upon which you rest. The night brings enjoyment almost as pleasant as that which was the recompense of the exertions of the day.

Having followed shooting for twenty-five years, mostly all through the different seasons, and sometimes camped out as much as three months at a time, never sleeping in a house during that period, I believe I have a sound and extensive practical

knowledge of the matters upon which this book is to treat. I am no scientific naturalist, and what I know has not been derived from books. I cannot give the Latin names of birds of game, waterfowl, snipe, woodcock, etc., and if I could you would not care about them, because the constant repetition of them makes no impression at all upon the sportsman. To him the quail is simply a quail, the pinnated grouse (commonly called prairie chicken) is a grouse, and no Latin is required to make him understand what you mean by a snipe or a woodcock. I cannot set down the scientific names by which naturalists distinguish the birds of which I shall treat, but I know their haunts and habits, and I can tell you when and where to seek them, and how to kill them in a sportsmanlike and satisfactory manner.

I was born in Albany County, New York, and began to shoot at fifteen years of age. I was then a tall, strong lad, and have since grown into a large, powerful, sinewy, and muscular man. I have always enjoyed fine health, had great strength and endurance, and been capable of much exertion and exposure. When 1 began to shoot, there was a good deal of game in Albany County, and it chiefly consisted of ruffed grouse and woodcock, which are difficult birds for young beginners. I received no instructions from anybody, but I possessed a quick, true eye, and steady nerve, and had, as I believe, the natural gifts which enable a man to become in time, with proper opportunity, a first-rate field shot. It was a long time after that before I ever shot at a pigeon from a trap, and I confess that I had for many years a strong prejudice against that sort of shooting. There were no quail, snipe, or ducks about Albany County at that time, and it was not until I removed to the West that I became familiar with them and with the pinnated grouse. Seventeen years ago I moved to Illinois, and settled on the Sangamon River, near Petersburg. It was more a broken, swampy country, with much cover, than a prairie land like that to the northwards in the State. Game of all sorts was in vast abundance. There were vast numbers of quail; the pinnated grouse were rather numerous, though nothing like as much so as upon some of the great prairies; ducks and geese came in immense flocks every spring and fall, and deer and turkeys abounded. It was, too, and is to this day, one of the best places for snipe that I know of. It was a paradise for a sportsman; and as for the snipe and quail, there was hardly a man there who could kill them except myself. Lots of men used to go out to see me shoot. There was one, a great hunter of deer and turkeys, with whom I became very intimate. At first he- laughed at me when he saw me loading with No. 8 shot. " That wunt kill nothin', stranger," said he. " What little I do at quail I do with No. 1 shot, and for prairie chicken I always use BBs. You can't stop 'em with anything lighter."

But he changed his opinion when he found by experience that I could kill ten to his one, and then it was the old story of the fox and grapes. " Darn the little creatures, I say!" he exclaimed; " I got no use for 'em anyhow!" At that time I used to stint myself in quail-shooting time to twenty-five brace a day. When I had got them, I gave over for the day. Often when I was shooting quail in the oak barrens two or three deer have got up close to me. I shot some turkeys; but my bag was mostly made up of quail and pinnated grouse in the fall, and of snipe in the spring. There were snipe in the fall too, but not so many. Ducks and geese were plentiful in the fall and spring, but I did not go after them much at that time. I had no wagon and team, and a bunch of ducks and geese is very heavy to carry. The country about the Sangamon was wild and very sparsely settled. Even now it has no large population, and remains a great resort for ducks and geese, a fine place for snipe, and the quail still abound. There was a fine variety of ducks. The bag would include mallards, bluebills, pintails, green-winged teal and blue-winged teal, with some wood-ducks. I consider the mallard the best duck we have in the West, and I doubt very much whether there is any better anywhere else. A great deal is said about the canvas-back, and with justice; but I do not think them any better eating than mallards are in the fall of the year, when they come on large and fat and glorious in plumage from the wild rice-fields of the northwest, away in the British territories.

After staying on the Sangamon about two years I moved to Elkhart, in Logan County, where I have lived ever since. It is in the heart of the State of Illinois, a hundred and sixty-six miles south of Chicago, eighteen miles northwest of Springfield, and one hundred and fifteen miles from St. Louis. It was then a grand place for game, and is very good now late in the fall, when the pinnated grouse pack and partially migrate. Fifteen years ago the prairies there were but sparsely settled, and not one acre in a thousand had been broken up. The grouse were in immense numbers ; the quail, though, were not as plentiful as on the Sangamon in the brushy land of the oak barrens. There was, however, and is now, a grove of timber six hundred acres in extent, not far from the town. It is one of the finest in the State, and in it and on its borders there were many quail. This grove was then owned and still belongs to Mr. John D. Gillot. He has a great stock-farm, his pasture-land running for seven miles at a stretch. Being a man of great enterprise, as well as large means, he planted hedges all over this estate. They have now grown up, and, affording harbor and nesting-places for the quail, the latter are now more plentiful in that neighborhood than they were when I first went to live there. At that tHfe very few in those parts used the double- barrelled gun, and shot over dogs. I was about the only one who followed shooting systematically and thoroughly. But though the quail in that neighborhood are now very abundant, they are hard to kill. The corn grows very tall, and as soon as a bevy is flushed away they go for the corn-fields. Once in them, with the stalks stand-

ing thick and high above your head, you can only kill birds by snap shots such as you make at woodcock in thick cover. You can find them on the stubbles and in the pastures at the right time of day, but when you have fired your two barrels at them they are off to the corn. The pin- nated grouse lie in the corn and on the borders of it a good deal too. There was no trouble in killing a great number when I first went there. I have known sixty young ones to be killed in a morning in one field, not more than a quarter of a mile from Elkhart. For my part, I am very much opposed to such doings. The commencement of the shooting season ought to be fixed by law a month later. When the shooting begins, the birds are very young, though of good size, and do not fly either fast or far; the weather is hot, and I am satisfied that above half of those which are killed are spoiled and never used. At I the present time the grouse are much more scarce about Elkhart, especially young grouse. The chief reason is the want of good nesting-places. Except in Mr. Gillot's extensive pastures, there are no good nesting-places left of any account. This is what causes the great diminution of the numbers of pinnated grouse. They are so prolific, and

their food is so abundant, tnat they could stand shooting in and out of season, and even the trapping and netting which are so extensively carried on in many parts; but when the prairie is all or nearly all broken up, no good breeding-places remain, and young grouse are not to be found. Thus it has been in a great measure about Elkhart. Late in the fall, when they pack and come in from the distant prairies where they breed, the birds seem to be as plentiful or nearly as plentiful as they were before. About the last of October and in November you may see as many as five hundred in a pack. They are then strong and wild. Some people maintain that the pinnated grouse do not migrate from one place to another. I am certain that with us they do. There are now ten times as many about Elkhart in November as there are in September, therefore the bulk of them are not bred there. Moreover, I have been at Keokuk in Iowa late in the fall, and have seen the grouse coming from the interior of that State in large numbers, and flying across the Mississippi River into Illinois. They are never known to do so at any other season, and if that is not migration .1 do not know what it can be. The river there is so wide that the flight

across is a long one for a grouse, and I think nothing but the migratory instinct would induce the grouse to make it, unless it were pressing danger. Now they face the danger in order to make their migration, for the people shoot at them as they fly over the town to cross the river, and some arc killed. I think they no doubt cross the Mississippi at many other points to make the east bank, and no one ever sees them return to Iowa. Ducks and geese are not so plentiful about Elkhart as they are on the San- gamon. Still their numbers are very large at times. They come out in the evening to feed in the cornfields, and at such times 1 have often killed twenty couple, which is a pretty good bag for one gun. Snipe are now scarce in the neighborhood of Elkhart. Cultivation and the draining of swamplands have converted the places which were the favorite resorts for snipe into the best wheat and corn land in the State. The change of condition in the land is the chief cause of the diminution of game of various sorts in particular places. It has more to do with it than all other causes. Although the pinnated grouse are trapped and netted by thousands, as well as shot in a sportsmanlike manner, it would not of itself reduce their numbers so E,s to be greatly perceptible. Immense numbers are sent East which are taken in nets and traps. Some are killed by coming in contact with the telegraph wires in their flight. But all these causes would be inadequate to reduce the stock much if the breeding birds had the nesting-places which they formerly used. The grouse used to breed in the prairies, commonly along the edges of the sloughs. In many parts the prairies are nearly all broken up and brought under cultivation. Many now make their nests in the fields of the farmer, and these nests are nearly all broken up and destroyed by the ploughing in the spring. Quail, whose nests are made in hedges and corners of fences and under bunches of brambles, escape, and we see them increase in numbers in the very places where the grouse diminish. A great source of destruction to the nests of the grouse might be easily prevented. In most places there are patches of prairie left for pasture, and in these the birds build. Many farmers follow a practice of burning these patches over late in the spring, under a notion that it improves the pasturage by causing the young grass to spring up fine and succulent as soon as the weather gets warm. When these patches of prairie are burnedover, there are commonly many nests in each, sometimes scores of them, and they are half-full of eggs. This cuts up the supply of grouse root and branch, and reduces the numbers to a serious extent every year. It is a great mistake on the part of the farmers, for the grouse, by consumption of grasshoppers and other destructive insects, is one of the agriculturist's best friends, and the grass would be just as good if the patches of prairie were burned over late in the fall, when there would be no nests destroyed. It is to be hoped that this plan will be adopted for the future ; and I think it will be, for the possession of guns and sporting-dogs, and the love of shooting, are spreading among the farmers of the West, and these, after all, will be in time the most efficient preservers of the game. The men, such as myself, who go every fall to shoot in the great unbroken prairies which still exist in Ford County, Champagne County, and about there, burn the grass themselves late in the fall, and thus leave nothing to be burned the following spring in nesting-time. By this means the stock of grouse is fully kept up, and it is from thence the great packs migrate towards the last of October and in November. Upon this subject I consider myselfcompetent to speak. I have had much experience, and have conferred with many practical men whose experience is nearly or quite as great as my own. What I have stated I know to be true. No doubt, when the hen-birds have lost their first nests by the plough, or by the much more destructive burning of the prairie patches late in spring, they make other nests; but these also are often destroyed; and if they are not, the broods are small and late, and quite unable to take care of themselves when the shooting season begins.

The best spring shooting in Illinois is snipe; and in many parts, such as that on the Sangamon Eiver, the birds are found in abundance. I know of no better ground for them anywhere. After the snipe come the golden plover, sometimes jn very large flocks. This beautiful and delicious little bird stays with us some three or four weeks, and the sport they afford is excellent. They are commonly shot from horseback, or by means of a wheeled vehicle, as is said to be the practice in the Eastern States. You must be a good sportsman to fill your bag with them, and there is no better practice for a good shot than at them. After remaining with us about a month the golden plover go farther north to breed. The up

land or gray plover stays with us and breeds in Illinois. They flock to some extent, but not in such large numbers as the golden plover do. I have often seen as many as four hundred or five hundred of the latter together, and they sometimes fly so close in the pack that a great many can be cut down with two barrels when you can get within fair distance. After they have scattered and run before they fly, the practice at the single birds is as good as anything for the education of a marksman. The upland plover are more open in their flight, as well as in smaller flocks. They ought not to be shot at all in the spring with us, for they do not arrive from the South until about corn-planting time, and then they are ready to pair and make their nests. September is the proper month to shoot them. They are then very fat and delicious for the table. They frequent the great pasture I mentioned belonging to Mr. Gillot. When Miles Johnson of New Jersey was in Illinois shooting with me over that ground, he said he had never seen such plover as those beforelthat is, for size and fatnessland that each of them would fetch half a dollar in Boston market.

Eight or ten years ago the American hare,

commonly called the rabbit, used to abound about Elkhart. I and another man, by beating the hedges, one on each side, after the first snow, when there was about four inches on the ground, once killed a hundred and sixty in a day. They decreased at one time, but recently they have been getting numerous again, and there is now a good head of them. The abundance of game in any given year depends very much upon the breeding season, for there are commonly old ones left to raise a good stock. If the spring is warm and moderately dry, the broods of quail and grouse are large, and the young birds grow up strong, so as to be able to fly fast and go a good distance when the shooting season begins. When the spring is cold and wet, many broods are lost through the nests being drowned out. The broods which are hatched out are small, and the young birds have a hard time of it until : summer begins. The last spring was a very favorable one in the West, and grouse and quail are numerous and strong. Farmers who had seen many nests of grouse told me that in most instances every egg had been hatched out, and in June I saw myself as many as twelve young grouse in a gang. All the old ones that I observed had large numbers of young birds, and the latter were large and strong. The Western country abounds with hawks, and these persecute the quail, grouse, and duck very much. I have seen a bevy of quail in such desperate terror when pursued by a hawk that they dashed against a house and many were killed. I kill all the hawks I can, and often let a grouse go unshot at in order to bring down a hawk. There is one bird of that order which makes great ravages among the ducks. It just kills for the sake of killing, for it strikes down one after the other. It is a small, long-winged hawk, very muscular and strong, and uncommonly rapid in flight. I have seen this hawk when pursuing ducks strike one down and let it lie, going on after the others, and continuing to harass and kill until the prey could reach water. This hawk does not consume a fourth of the grouse and duck it kills. It is not large enough to carry away a good-sized duck, and I doubt whether it could fly away with a grouse for any distance. Eighty miles from Elk- hart there is the Winnebago Swamp, a large and wild track of water, moss, and cover. Ducks, such as mallard, teal, and widgeon, breed there in large numbers. I have often flushed themfrom their nests when I have been snipe-shooting thereabout. A few geese breed there also, but perhaps these are only those which, owing to being wounded or to some accident, have been unable to join the great flocks in their spring flight towards the North. From what I am told by men who have been explorers and hunters in the service of the Hudson's Bay Company, no matter how far north Indians or white men may penetrate, it is found that the geese go farther in the summer, and bring back their broods in the fall. In this Winnebago Swamp I have occasionally found the nest of the sand-hill crane, and sometimes that of the blue crane. The crane builds its nest on the top of a muskrat house, just as the geese do in that section. It lays two eggs, much larger than those of a goose, especially in length, and one of the cranes commonly keeps watch by the nest. The nests of the ducks are built on tussocks of grass. The Winnebago Swamp used to harbor many wolves, and there are a considerable number there yet. Three years ago, in company with a hunter named Henry Conderman, I found the den of a she-wolf in the swamp, and we took her litter of six whelps. Afterwards we trapped the old one. We got thirty-five dollarsfrom the county, as it pays a bounty of five dollars a head. The gray prairie wolf is very destructive of young pigs, lambs, geese, etc., and wolves are more numerous in Illinois now than most people suppose. Last spring Mr. Gillot took a litter of five whelps in his grove near Elkhart. He has a grand wolf-hunt every summer. The men who have hounds in the neighborhood meet, and a small pack is got together, with which we hunt the grove, and there is nearly always fine sport. Mr. Gillot's daughters have fine saddle-horses and are good riders. With some other ladies they see the chase from the hills, and there is a grand time. Last summer we ran three down in the pastures and killed them. Another also took to the open, and was killed after the hunt was over in one of the pastures by Mr. L. B. Dean. Thus there were four accounted for, all of one litter and about half- grown. But the old wolves got away, as they usually do, for our hounds are not able to run on to an old wolf. They go very fast, keep up their lope for a long time, know the ground well, and are very cunning as well as fierce when cornered or brought to bay. Gray foxes are numerous with us. Eagles are commonly to befound along the creeks, and they are sometimes very bold. Last winter one made a sudden pounce and grabbed a grouse I had just shot. 1 gave him the No. 6 shot from the other barrel, and as he was near I expected to see him fall, but he got away with the charge without the grouse.

From that which has been stated in this introductory chapter, it will be apparent that there is no trouble in finding places where good shooting may be had. Even where there are no. pinnated grouse, the sportsman may find plenty of work for his dogs and his gun. It is not to be expected that, in parts very thickly settled and populated, there will be the abundance and variety of game which might once be found. Many snipe-grounds are now drained, and some are even thickly built over. The brakes and thickets which once held the woodcock have largely been cut up and cleared away. Quail, however, are more numerous in many States than they ever were before. The shooting at them is excellent in most of the counties of Ohio, Indiana, Illinois, Kentucky, Iowa, Missouri, Wisconsin, and Minnesota. Northern Indiana and Michigan are also famous for snipe and duck, as Illinois, Iowa, Missouri, andMinnesota are. Perhaps the best general shooting is to be had in Northeastern Missouri, for there, besides grouse, quail, waterfowl, etc., the sportsman may come upon wild turkeys and deer, and the same is true of some parts of Iowa. Of the best places for game in the Eastern States I am not so well acquainted, and I shall, therefore, say but little about them. This book is mainly to relate the results of my own experience, not to gather up and adopt what others may know.

2

SECTION 2

CHAPTER II.
  GUNS AND THEIR PROPER CHARGES.
  I cotrtD never see any use to the shooter in a long theoretical or practical description of the principles and details of guns as they are made. All such knowledge is necessary to the gunmaker, but of no practical use at all to the shooter, for which reason I shall say next to nothing about it. It is no more essential to the marksman or young sportsman that he should understand the mechanism and mode of manufacturing guns, than it is that he should determine whether the Chinese or Roger Bacon first invented gunpowder before he shall fire a shot off. Sportsmen may safely leave such matters to the gunmakers, who are nearly everywhere a very ingenious, painstaking, trustworthy class of men. There is no handicraft in which more care is displayed or more ambition felt to excel. The improvements and ingenious devices which have so rapidly followed one another of late years, all proceeding from members of H
  the art and mystery of gunmaking, establish this beyond doubt. There are plenty of men among us who can remember when nothing was in use but the old flint-lock gun. They have not forgotten the misfires which often occurred, when the sportsman was left staring after the bird, which flew away rejoicing, and impartially distributing his curses between the flint, the lock, and the priming. The percussion-lock with its

detonating cap was an immense improvement, and, no doubt, suggested the use in the household of the friction- matches which have quite superseded the old- fashioned tinder-box with its piece of flint and steel. Then came the breech-loader, an invention of enormous value, and so much improved upon since its first discovery and application that upon this principle, with various details of construction for opening, shutting, and securing the piece at the breech, the most convenient, the safest, and the best guns in the world are now made. A few- years ago many good sportsmen would have disputed this statement, and there are some who will do so now. It is, however, founded upon large experience and many trials of the breech-loader in my own hands, against the most vaunted muzzle- loaders in those of other good marksmen andsportsmen. I was for some time after breech-loading guns came out of a contrary opinion, but results convinced me of my error. Results always convince reasonable men|that is to say, a great preponderance of results. When such a man has held a cherished opinion upon what seems to be sufficient grounds, he does not abandon it all at once because something happens which seems to tell against it. He tries the matter again and again, and when, after a large number of trials, there is a great preponderance of results against his preconceived opinion, he changes it. Now the fool never changes his. No matter what happens, the obstinate blockhead will not admit of change in consequence of discovery. His motto is, " What I says I stands to !"

I first began to shoot with an old musket|flintlock, of course, and probably one of those specimens of " Brown Bess" which had been used in wars against the French and Indians before the Revolution. I was then a boy, and soon found out that for the game about Albany County, New York, " Brown Bess" would not do. As soon as by hard work and careful saving I had got together twenty-five dollars (twenty-five dollars was rather hard to get in those days) I bought a muzzle-loader. It was a

cheap gun, and I do not recommend cheap guns; but when a man cannot afford an expensive one, a cheap gun is a good deal better than none,. or than an old " Brown Bess" musket. For some years after I went to Illinois as well as before, I never shot with any but common guns. I killed plenty of game, and could always sell a gun when it was pretty well worn out for as much as I had paid for it. Men looking at the size of the bunch of grouse or ducks I brought in, or at the twenty brace of quail to which I stinted myself in the oak barrens on the Sangamon, thought it was the gun which accounted for the success, and were ready to buy it. Afterwards I got a Greener gun, one of the best muzzle-loaders that I have ever seen. I paid one hundred and twenty-five dollars for it, and it had but one fault. It weighed seven pounds and a half, which is too light for my estimate of excellence. It kicked when pretty heavily charged, and kept my finger and cheek sore. But it was a close-shooting, hard-hitting gun, and when the breech-loaders came out I would not have swapped it for a hundred of them. I thought they would not put their shot regular and close, and that they would lack penetration. I have since completely changed that opinion. I was then ready to shoot

with the Greener gun against any man with a breechloader, and would have laid all the money I could raise that I beat him in the field and at the traps. I might possibly have done so, for I have never yet met a man who could beat me in field-shooting, but the breech-loading gun would not have been the cause of my opponent's defeat.

My opinion of breech-loaders now is, that they excel muzzle-loaders in three or four particulars of the very greatest importance. Of course I speak of good guns. In the first place, they put the shot closer and distribute them more evenly than muzzle-loaders do. Some sportsmen will say " No !" I should myself have said No once, and so would several other noted marksmen I can name who were afterwards convinced by me against their wills, and now use no guns but breech-loaders. A breech-loader will also shoot as hard as a muzzle-loader, provided you use a little more powder. My breech-loading guns have shot harder than any muzzle-loading gun I ever tested them against, but I used a dram more powder, and of fine quality at that. I think I was the first man who ever stepped up to shoot a championship match at pigeons with a breech-loading gun. It was against Ira Paine, on Long Island. I was defeated in the match, but it was not thefault of the gun. I liked that so well that 1 agreed to shoot at one hundred birds every day for a week against Paine; each day's match to be independent of the othersla hundred birds each for five hundred dollars. We shot the first of the six, but as I killed eighty to Paine's sixty-two he paid forfeit on the other matches. Since then I have used breech-loaders altogether, whether for match-shooting or in the field. Besides the superiority of their shooting, the quickness of the shots when you come upon birds in the field which lie well is a very material advantage. The greater ease with which the ammunition is carried is another; and the cleanliness and complete absence of danger in loading is a further great point. Many accidents formerly occurred in the loading, of muzzle-loaders. And . I must say this for the gunmakers, even when cheap muzzle-loaders were in use, not one accident in a hundred, in my experience, was owing to defects in the barrels of the guns. Of the few which burst, nine out of ten were either improperly loaded or the charge had partly shifted before the trigger was pulled. The fact is now and always was, that the vast majority of accidents with guns are not caused by bad guns, but by bad handling of guns which are good enough

for anybody's use. Another great thing in favor of the breech-loader is its certainty in wet and damp weather; there are no misfires on that account. The first cost of a breech-loader is somewhat larger than that of a muzzle-loader of equal goodness and finish. Formerly the cost of ammunition made it dearer to use, but the employment of metallic cartridge-cases has changed that. They can be used over and over again, and I have used some above a hundred times. Thus the expense of ammunition has been largely reduced. There has, too, been a great reduction of late in the price of good, strong, exact-shooting breech-loading guns, and they will, no doubt, soon supersede muzzle- loaders altogether. Many of the superb, highly- finished and fitted guns are sold, but if a man can. not afford to go to the highest price, he can find good serviceable weapons for less money. Still, as a good gun will last a man the greater part of a lifetime, it is well to buy the best you can really afford when you are about the business. A serviceable breech-loader can now be got for a hundred dollars; but where you have means pay more money for a better finished, and perhaps truer and more durable, article. I shoot with a gun of ten gauge, thirty-two inches in the barrels, and ten pounds weight. This is a gun for all sorts of uses. It will stop anything that flies or runs on this side of the Kocky Mountains, if properly charged and aimed. Many may think ten pounds too heavy to carry, but the advantage of a good solid gun in delivery

of fire is very great. I do not like light guns, neither muzzle-loaders nor breech-loaders. The breechloader I am now using was a three-hundred-dollar gun, and, considering the prices they were selling at when I bought it, was worth the money. It has done a great deal of work|much hard work |and done it well. I have shot with it twelve times in matches against time, undertaking to kill fifty birds in eight minutes, and have won the money every time. I have also killed with it fifty-three out of fifty-four birds in four minutes and forty-five seconds. This was at Jersey- ville, Illinois, twenty .yards from the trap and two birds in the trap. H. B. Slayton .was present. At New Orleans I killed one hundred and eleven out of one hundred and eighteen in seventeen minutes and thirty seconds, and picked up my own birds. I have shot many other matches with this gun, besides using it in a vast amount of field-shooting every spring, fall, and winter. All this work it has stood well. It has never been to a gunsmith-shop to be repaired, and is as tight at the breech and as perfect in the opening and clasping action as ever it was. These facts prove conclusively that there is nothing wrong in the principle of a breech-loader, and that, if such a gun is properly constructed, it will stand as much wear and tear as a muzzle-loader. I am, however, of the opinion that shooting the time-matches has somewhat impaired the fine shooting qualities of this gun by making the barrels so hot. I fancy it does not now throw its shot so close or distribute it so evenly as it did before the barrels were heated in these matches. They got so hot that the resin broiled out of the soldered joints along the rib, and in one instance burned my hand through a buckskin glove. To shoot well, a man must have his gun so stocked as to fit him. Some require a longer stock than others. Some like stocks which are nearly straight, while others can shoot with a gun the stock of which is crooked. It depends mostly on the build of the man. A long-armed man does not want a gun with a short stock. A man with a moderately long neck cannot use a gun which is straight in the stock with ease or pleasure. I choose a stock of moderate length, and one that is rather crooked|one with a drop of about three inches. This sort of a gun comes even up to the shoulder with most men, and you do not have to crook the neck much in taking aim with -it. Some people protend that there is no need to look along the rib at the bird in order to shoot well. They shoot well, and they say they do not do so. I believe they are mistaken. Taking aim does not mean dwelling on
 . i the aim and pottering about in an uncertain way

with the gun at the shoulder. Even in snipe- shooting there is a distinct aim taken, though, when a good-fitting gun is brought up to the shoulder, the aim is almost instantaneous, and the discharge follows on the next instant. At pigeons some men do shoot without sighting the bird; but they know just where the bird must fly from, and they have the trick of covering the trap by raising the breech and lowering the muzzle as if done "by a gauge, and then they blaze away. Such men often kill the bird before it gets on the wing, and this proves that practically they shoot at the trap and just beyond it, rather than at the bird. This sort of thing is impracticable in the field, and there, if not everywhere else, the man who sights his bird along the rib of his gun, in shooting straight forward, makes the best bag. There are, of course, some situations in which you must practise snap-shooting to get any shooting at all. At woodcock in cover, or at grouse and quail in corn, you can have but a glimpse of the bird you shoot at, and you must aim just where intuition, as it may be called, tells you the bird will be. In cases where the bird can be plainly seen it should be Distinctly aimed at. It is not a question of quickness. In the time-matches where I must necessarily shoot very quick, and In those matches where I stand between two traps forty yards apart, which are pulled at the same time, I sight my bird before I pull the trigger. If I did not, I could never accomplish the feats which have become easy to me.

There are still many men prejudiced against breech-loading guns, and some who have given them a trial remain so. But in most of these latter cases the men have either got hold of a poor gun, or do not know how to load a good one. If the cartridge is not properly filled, wadded, and turned down, the shooting will be inferior, no matter how good the gun may be or how skilful the shooter. Last April I saw a match shot at Frank-

fort, Kentucky, in which one man used a breechloader and the other a muzzle-loader. As soon as they began to shoot I saw that the breech-loader, although it was in the hands of the best man of the two, would be beaten. And why? Because his cartridges were not properly filled. The wads on the powder, instead of lying flat and snug, were often partly edgewise. It was the same with the wads on the shot, besides which the cartridges were not well turned down over the wads. The shooter who had lost the match blamed his gun, which was a light one, and sent for one of ten pounds weight, Ifle mine. But if he is as careless in loading his cartridges for the heavy gun as he was when he had the light one, the shooting will not be any better. I could have told him how to win, but it was not my business to interfere in the matter. The shot in the cartridges should have been taken out, the wads sent home true, and the ends of the cases turned down close after the shot was replaced and evenly wadded.

The first time 1 visited New York and other Eastern States for the purpose of pigeon-shooting I spent some days with Miles Johnson, of Yard- ville, Mercer County, New Jersey. He is a famous pigeon-shooter and an excellent field sportsman. Few men, if any, know better how, when, and where to make a good bag of woodcock, snipe, or quail. Now, Miles had a number of crack muzzle-loaders, expressly for shooting-matches, and he was confident no breech-loader could equal them in pattern and penetration. I remarked that I had a good gun, and would shoot against him and his best muzzle-loader at a target. Miles declared with some heat and vociferation that " he'd be !" if I could beat him in shooting at a target at all, let alone using a breech-loader against the most famous of his muzzle-loaders. However, taking paper for targets and our guns, we repaired to an old barn near Yardville, and shot at them. Mr. Nathan Dorsey was present. I beat Miles very easily, and with an ounce of shot put more pellets in the target from the breechloader than he did with an ounce and a half from his muzzle-loader. Miles hardly knew what to make of it, but, perceiving that the penetration of my shot was also good, he finally acknowledged that a good breech-loader would beat any other sort of gun in shooting, and he now shoots with one himself. And thus it will be found in almost every case. When a man has strong preconceived opinions, it is of very little use to arguewith him. The effectual thing is to show him that he is in error by actual demonstration of the facts in his presence. Nothing but actual experience would have convinced me at one time that a breech-loader would shoot as well as, or better than, a first-rate muzzle-loader. Now I know the fact. I convinced Abraham Kleinman, of Calumet, Illinois, in the same practical manner He is, in my opinion, the best duck-shooter in the country, and one of the best at pigeons from the trap. His brothers, John and Henry, are also good shots. They had used muzzle-loaders all their lives, and could not be persuaded that breech loaders were good until Abraham found that I could beat him and use one. He then got one himself, and John and Henry soon followed his example. Nearly all the good shots in Illinois now prefer the breech-loading gun. Some held out against it for a long time on the ground that it was new!as if every good thing which is old had not been new itself one time. Not very long ago the percussion- lock was new. Again, some people have a prejudice as to breech loaders, believing them to be defective in the very points wherein they excel. On the seventh and eighth of last April I shot at Frankfort, Kentucky, for sweepstakes. All thesubscribers except myself had muzzle-loading guns. It was a wet, damp day, and my opponents had got it into their heads that the breechloader would often miss fire in such weather. They therefore insisted upon a change in their rules so as to provide that when the gun missed fire it should be a lost bird, no matter how well the gun might have been loaded. I must admit that I chuckled inwardly as I agreed to this change. I knew the weather might affect their caps, but that it could not impair mine in the cartridges. We shot the first day; the muzzle-loaders missed fire several times, while my breechloader never missed fire at all. The upshot of it was that for the second day's shooting they demanded the repeal of the new rule, so that they could have another bird after a misfire, if the gun was properly loaded and capped. I could, of course, have resisted this demand effectually; for when in such a case action has begun, there can be no change in rules or conditions without the unanimous consent of all concerned as principals. But I agreed to the change, and won both stakes. A good breech-loader will shoot as well in wet weather as in fair weather, and there will be no misfires on account of damp. But if there is adefect in the action of the plunger, so that it does not strike square on the cap, there will be misfires in any weather. This is a point which needs particular attention in the choice of a gun. As I said before, I shoot with a gun of ten pounds weight now, and prefer it much to those of seven and a half pounds, with which I used to shoot formerly. But some think a gun of ten pounds too heavy to carry through a long day and use in all sorts of ground. For many a lighter gun would be better for woodcock-shooting, and for grouse and quail in tall corn. But I would not recommend any one to get a gun of less weight than seven and a half pounds for general shooting and good service. If in choosing a gun you are in doubt concerning the weight which will suit you, give *the gun* the benefit of it, and take one a pound heavier than you have had before, if it weighed seven and a half pounds or less. A man soon gets used to the extra pound in the weight of his gun, and carries and uses it as easily as he did the lighter one, while the shooting of it will be much nicer and more pleasant, and the bag of game will be larger. The question is one of convenience, hardly of strength; for any man fit to go into the field at all can carry and use a gunof eight pounds weight. It is true that until men have worked themselves into some condition they will get tired in tramping over the prairies and fields and through the coverts carrying such a gun, but so they would if they carried nothing but a cane.

    In loading a gun of ten gauge for grouse I put into my cartridges four and a half or five drams of powder and an ounce of No. 9 shot, in the early part of the season. Later on I use No. 8 shot, and still later No. 7. In November and December, for the shooting of grouse and duck, I charge with No. 6. Some use larger shot for ducks, but a charge of No. 6 from a good gun, well held, will stop a duck as far off as seventy yards sometimes. With a strong charge of powder and shot of moderate size there is greater penetration, and a better chance of hitting besides. When I go out expressly for brant and geese, I load my cartridges with No. 2; but when out for general shooting, I have killed many brant and some geese with No. 6. For quail-shooting I use No. 8 or No. 9; for plover, No. 8; for snipe, No. 10. For wild turkeys I once preferred shooting with a rifle, but I now use the breech-loading shot-gun with No. 1 shot in the cartridges. With such a gun and ammunition I have killed as many as eleven in one forenoon. For field- shooting and match-shooting I have hitherto used what is called Dead Shot powder, and have found it very good. I have, however, since given a thorough test to the Orange Powder made by the Laflin and Rand Powder Company. I found the Orange Ducking and Orange Lightning Powder the best for giving penetration that I have used, and as good for making pattern as any. I shot it from my own gun, and can conscientiously and strongly recommend it. They make lower grades of powder nearly as good, but the sportsman had better buy the sorts mentioned. In champion matches I use paper cases for the cartridges, and put in five drams of powder, with two pink-edged wads over it. They must be forced down square and level upon the powder with a rammer, but not rammed too hard. An ounce and a half of No. 9 shot is then put in, evenly placed, and a thin wad, or the half of a split pink-edged wad, is pressed down firmly and evenly upon the shot. The cartridge is then to be turned down smoothly and closely on the upper wad. In matches and in field-shooting I always have used the shot made by Tatham & Brother, of New York, when it was possible to get it. When I shot the championship match against Abraham Kleinman, of Calumet, at Chicago, there was none of Tatham's shot of the right number in the city. Being determined to shoot with no other, if I could help it, I telegraphed to Detroit for a bag, and it was sent on by express in time for the shooting. I killed all my hundred birds, and only seven fell out of bounds. I decidedly prefer No. 9 shot to any other number at the trap. For field-shooting 1 employ metallic cartridge-cases; they shoot well and are cheap, as they can be used many times over. The paper ones shoot a little the best, but a bird or two in field-shooting is a mere nothing, and metal cases do well enough. I load them with five drams of powder and *one* pink- edged wad square down upon it, and the same as to the shot. I employ wads two sizes larger than the bore of the gun. Thus, for a ten-gauge gun, No. 8 wads. This is necessary to keep them firm, so that the charge may not start in one barrel when the other is fired. Even with the large, tight wads in the cartridges it is best to fire the barrels as nearly alternately as may be. It will not do to shoot one barrel four or five times with the charge in the other all the while.

1 believe there is nothing more needful to be said concerning guns, ammunition, and loading. It will have been seen that I believe in the necessity of large charges of good, strong powder more than in the efficacy of very large shot. The smaller shot, as I believe, are driven at higher velocities, and have greater penetration, than larger ones. Besides, the number of pellets to the weight of the charge is a very material thing. The more there are, the more will, in all probability, be put into the bird shot at.

But, as a matter of course, in following this principle a man is not to run into extremes and use very small shot for large game. On the other hand, he is not to be too ready, when the birds are not brought to bag, to lay it to the fault of small-sized shot. No shot is big enough to stop a bird without hitting him; and before changing the size of the shot or finding fault with the gun, it will be better to endeavor to mend and improve the aim.

3

SECTION 3

CHAPTER IIL
   PINNATED-GROUSE SHOOTINO.
   The pinnated grouse, commonly called prairie- chicken where it is most abundant in the West, is a handsome bird, weighing from two pounds to two and a half pounds, sometimes nearly three when it has reached mature size. It is a delicious bird on the table, cither when split and broiled while young, the flesh being then white, or roasted when of full size. It formerly prevailed in New Jersey, Pennsylvania, Long Island, and Kentucky, in parts where there were open heaths; but it is not now found until the valley of the Mississippi is reached. There are none in Ohio, but few in Indiana and Michigan; but it is plentiful in Illinois, Iowa, Minnesota, Kansas, Nebraska, and parts of Missouri and Wisconsin. The pinnated grouse is a bird of the grassy plains and great prairies, and does not frequent the woodland, save on frosty mornings, when it may be seen perched on trees near the edges of the groves. At such times, too, it will be seen perched on fences and corn-shocks. On such mornings, when the weather is still as well as chilly, the grouse may be heard cackling and chattering in tho timber-land for a considerable distance inwards, but on other occasions they never resort to the groves. This bird is certainly of much service to the agriculturist, as it consumes many grasshoppers and other destructive insects, while the little wheat, corn, and oats it

eats does not amount to anything by comparison. Indeed, its food, before the wheatland is in stubble, is probably wholly composed of insects and the buds of heather and other plants to be found in the prairies and in the spacious pastures of the West. Before the great prairies of Illinois and other Western States were broken up by the plough of the settler, the grouse were more numerous than they are now, and they could not have fed on grain, because there were no fields of grain within hundreds of miles of them. It is the same now in those parts where the prairies are still extensive, and on the great pastures whore droves of bullocks, hundreds strong in number, are fatted for the Eastern markets. It is my firm belief, from observations made for many years about the time of the breeding season, that the pinnated grouse is polygamous, like our domestic cOcks and hens. I have never seen them paired off as quail are. Early in the spring the cocks are together in gangs. They get on hilly places, swell out their necks, and make a booming noise, which can be heard at a considerable distance. At this time, too, they fight with each other like game-cocks. The hens at the same season are to be found in gangs, but not on the same ground as the cocks. While the latter congregate on the hills the hens remain on the prairie, and go into the corn-fields to feed. A great deal of corn remains standing all the winter in the West, and is not shucked until it is time to plough and plant again. The grouse mostly roost in the long grass of rich bottomlands. About the last of April and beginning of May the hens make their nests. I have found one on the tenth of May containing as many as eight eggs. The nest is made on the ground, and formed of a little grass, and is a good deal like that of a domestic hen when she makes one in the fields. When the hen-grouse can conveniently get to the prairie, they build in that grass. When they cannot, they build in the fields, and often in patches of weeds. In the bottoms, which are generally wet at that season, the nests are madeon tussocks of thick grass which rise above the surface. When the weather happens to be wet about the last of May, many nests in the bottomlands are overflowed, and the young which may have been hatched mostly perish by cold, starvation, or drowning. The hens which have had their nests destroyed by floods, by prairie-burning, or by the plough, commonly build again, but their broods are late, and usually of small number. The hen lays from twelve to eighteen eggs, white in color, and about the size of those of a bantam hen. The hen sets twenty-one days, the same as barn-door fowl. The young run as soon as hatched; and if a man or a dog should go near where they are, they will hide and skulk under the grass, even on the first day, while the old hen will try to lead the intruder away. They feed on insects for the most part, the old hens catching them at first for the young chicks. The latter, however, soon learn to catch them for themselves. As they grow larger, they feed a good deal on herbage. The young increase in size very rapidly. They are not hatched until early in June, at the earliest; and on the fourth of July, in a favorable season, I have seen broods which were half grown. The breeding-time varies according to the season and the situation, but every year there are some broods early, some late, and some very late, the latter being brought off by hens which have lost their first nests. By the fifteenth of August some of th broods are about full grown; but they are then tame, and, having grown so rapidly, are weak on the wing, and soon tire. I believe hybrids have been produced by the hen-grouse and the bantam cock. Last spring, at Omaha, Nebraska, I saw in the possession of Mr. George A. Hoagland,

President of the Shooting Club, a bird of the preceding year, which had been shot out of a covey of seven or eight. This bird was believed to be a hybrid. There was another of the same brood in the town, and both were well stuffed and set up. All the brood were alike as to markings and appearance. Their size was that of a grouse two-thirds grown. In shape they were more like the bantam or barn-door fowl than the grouse. The ground color of their plumage was a dingy white, but they were spangled all over with feathers colored and barred like those of grouse. That they were hatched by a hen-grouse is unquestionable, for she was often seen with them. She made her nest close to a house, and it was believed that a domestic cockwas the father of her young ones. Albinos of the grouse species are sometimes seen, but those above referred to were not at all like Albinos. There is a very beautiful specimen of the Albino at the Grand Central Hotel at Omaha, and the supposed hybrids did not resemble it in the least. 1 was informed that this brood of spangled grouse or hybrids were exceptionally wild. But for all that most of them were shot, though but two preserved. These birds are still to be seen at Omaha, and it might be well for a scientific naturalist to examine them.

The game-law of Illinois allows the shooting of grouse to commence on the fifteenth of August, and in some States it is suffered to begin as early as the first of that month. Both these dates are too early. The first of September would be quite soon enough, and most sportsmen would prefer that date. As the law now stands, nearly all begin to shoot early; for as some will do so, it cannot be expected that many others will refrain. On the fifteenth of August some broods of grouss are full grown, but the great majority are not, and many broods are not more than half grown, while some are so small as to be almost unable to fly. These are the broods of birds whose firstnests were broken up in the spring. I never shoot at these half-callow young, but there are plenty of people who do. The early-grouse shooting is very good practice for young beginners with, the gun, as they lie until you are near them, and fly slowly. But it would be just about as good if the shooting was deferred fifteen days later by law, as the birds would still lie close and fly slowly. The early shooting makes the birds wild before they would otherwise become so, and it brings many to the bag half grown that would, under other circumstances, be bagged full grown. In the early part of the season grouse-shooting in the West is the easiest there is. The birds lie well to the dogs, their flight is slow, and they can usually be marked down near at hand. There is, however, one thing which affords protection to the grouse, and presents considerable difficulty to the shooter. There are commonly corn-fields at no great distance, and if they fly into the corn when flushed in the stubbles or the prairie, it is very difficult to kill them. It is, on the whole, better to let them go as not attainable. Men cannot shoot well in tall corn; dogs can do but little in it, even the best of dogs, at that season, and young ones are utterly

useless, as they can neither see you nor you them, and no instructions can be given to them. The early season is the time for young beginners, as the broods are then numerous and easily found. If the shooting was not allowed before September, it would answer the purpose of teaching the novices quite as well; for though the birds would be somewhat stronger on the wing, they would lie just as close, and would be larger. After the broods have been shot at two or three weeks, they are thinned out considerably, and have become much wilder. They are then of fine size, the weather has become cooler, and the birds can be kept. At least half of the young grouse killed in the month of August become spoiled and are never used. Some may doubt this, but I state what I know to be facts. In August the weather is very often close and sultry; for though there is commonly some air on the wide prairies, the breezes do not then prevail.

At the beginning of the shooting season the grouse will be found at early morning in the stubbles. They have gone out of their roosting-placcs to feed in the stubbles of the wheat and oat fields, which have then been pretty well overgrown with rag-weed, and afford thick cover. Where flax iscultivated, you may look for them in the flax stubbles, as they are some of their most favorite resorts. Another good place to beat, whenever you see one, is a bean-patch. The navy bean is a good deal cultivated in Illinois and Iowa, and the grouse resort to the patches. About nine or ten o'clock, when the sun has got high and the morning hot, the grouse leave the stubbles and bean-patches, and walk into the long prairie-grass or into the corn. On such days, in clear weather, at that season of the year, it is best to give over shooting about ten o'clock, and lie by until late in the afternoon, when you may pursue your sport again with prospects of success, and fill up your bag. To continue after the grouse in the middle of the day is merely to distress your dogs and to fatigue yourself for nothing. There is no scent, and the grouse will not lie in the open prairie. But on damp, cloudy days the case is altogether different. The birds then remain in the stubbles all day, unless flushed and driven into the corn; the dogs can work and scent better; and under these overcast skies are the best and most glorious days of the grouse-shooter in the early part of the season. Later in the fall and at the beginning of winter the habit of the grouse iadifferent, as will be specially noticed further on. A cloudy day, cool air, the dogs feeling and working well, plenty of grouse in the stubbles, and the sportsman out of the glaring sunshine and able to shoot deliberately and well, make great enjoyment and a good bag. On the clear days, when the grouse have left the stubbles for the prairie-grass and corn, instead of shooting all the time until you are tired, as you will be before night, until you have been seasoned and got into hard condition of muscle and wind, lay off in some house, or your camp, or in your wagon in the shade, if you can find it, until about four or half- past four o'clock in the afternoon. Then it will be time to begin to beat the stubbles again. The grouse will have come, or will be coming, on to them again from the resorts in which they spent the hot hours of the day; and you and your dogs, being refreshed and rested, will be in good fettle for the sport. The sun will get low, and finally go down over the distant swells of land to the westward; the dew will begin, insensibly to you, to fall; the dogs will find the birds easily, they will lie well, and you may shoot as long as you can see in the twilight.

Ift some parts of Illinois, Iowa, and otherWestern States there are very extensive ranges of pasture-land, on which great herds of cattle, many from Texas, are fattened. These lands have not been broken up by the plough at any time, but, being regularly depastured, have lost much of the prairie character. They remain, however, good resorts for grouse, and the shooting over them is some of the best to be had. The grouse bred on them probably never see a stubble-field, at least until after late in the fall of their first year. Their habits are the same as those of the birds which are found near the arable corn, wheat, and oat lands. In the morning they will be found on the ridges and knolls where the grass is short. In the heat of the day they retire into the long grass which abounds in low, moist places. In the evening they return to the knolls and ridges again. These pastures are sometimes of the extent of two thousand acres or more, and the shooting on them is second to none in those States. Yet they are comparatively little shot over, especially in the early part of the season. As a rule, it is believed the grouse are more abundant where the land is varied and stubbles, pieces of prairie, corn-fields, and patches of beans are found in the immediate neighborhoodof each other. For this reason most of the sportsmen, especially those of the towns near at hand, or from the more distant cities, who shoot mostly in the early part of the season, go to them, and do not attempt the wide pastures. But give me the sport on the latter, and let me begin about the middle of September, when most of the grouse bred on them are full-grown, strong birds, coming down with a thump seemingly hard enough to make a hole in the ground when killed clean and well. The grouse in these places commonly lie first-rate to the dog, and get up by twos and threes, so that a good shot has a chance to bring to bag many of the covey, and those he cannot shoot at the first rise may be easily marked down. In 1872 Miles Johnson of New Jersey was shooting with me in McLean County, Illinois. We camped near Bell- flower, and had a man for camp-keeper while Miles and I shot. We were out ten days, and in that time bagged six hundred grouse, shooting only mornings and evenings. As I have said before, and wish to impress particularly upon my readers for their information and advantage, it is of no use to try for grouse in the middle of the day, when the weather is clear, in the early partof the fall. The best day Miles Johnson and I had that time was in one of the great pastures 1 have alluded to above. It contained from five to ten thousand acres. We went into it early in the morning, and came out about eleven o'clock in the forenoon with eighty full-grown grouse. That was a capital morning's sport, no doubt, but I have often had as good.

While we were at the camp near Bellflower we were visited by Johnson's friend, Mr. Eldridge of New Jersey. With him came Dr. Goodbreak of Clinton, Illinois. The doctor is an army surgeon and an ardent and excellent sportsman. They shot with us two days, using muzzle-loaders; but when Dr. Goodbreak had seen the execution I did with my breech-loader, sometimes getting two or three nice shots while one was loading, and often killing a long way off, he was satisfied as to which was the best style of gun, and sent an order for a breech-loader to cost three hundred and fifty dollars. After being there ten days Miles Johnson left for home. I remained at the camp, and in a while A. Leslie and H. Robinson of Elkhart carne up and shot with me. It was then getting late in the fall, and we had excellent success. The grouse were wild and very fast on the wing. They werestrong, and it took good shooting and hard hitting to bring thorn to the bag. I killed from ten brace to twenty brace a day, and averaged about fifteen brace. My companions together did not secure as many. In shooting grouse on the .pastures, and indeed anywhere, you should beware of shooting too soon. Many more birds are missed at short than at long shots, in my opinion. The sudden, loud whirr made by the rising of the grouse when it gets up startles young sportsmen, and some nervous, excitable old ones too. The shot is hastily delivered, while the bird is so near that the charge has not distance enough to diverge and spread in, and the game is often missed. If the shooter had waited for steady sight of the bird along the rib, which is not to be a slow, pottering aim, it would have been often brought down. In McLean County, Ford County, and the others of the tier on that line, there is as good grouse-shooting as any I know of anywhere in Illinois. They are in the section of country lying southwest of Chicago, and a line drawn from that city to St. Louis in Missouri would pass through them. As good places as any to get *off* the railroad at are Bellflower in McLean County, and Gibson in Ford County. Twelve miles from Gibson is the great farm of Mr. Michael Sullivant, formerly of Columbus, Ohio. He has a tract of land containing forty-five thousand acres. It is a splendid place to shoot, and real sportsmen are made welcome by the owner. I was there last spring after brant and ducks, and made heavy bags. I saw at that time large numbers of grouse la powerful breeding-stock.

In shooting over the great pastures I have mentioned particular care must be taken not to go near the herds of cattle. They are pretty wild, and the coming near them of dogs makes them excited. In the first plape, the farmers do not like to have dogs taken near their cattle, and every good sportsman should carefully avoid doing anything which may annoy the owners of the land on which he may be. I can always get along pleasantly with the owners of the land, and so may any one else who will use them well and refrain from damage. In the second place, if shooting parties go near the great herds of cattle with their dogs, the bullocks will come for the latter at a run in a big drove, the frightened dogs will run to their masters, and before the men can get out of the way of the furiousrush they may be knocked down, trampled over by scores of hoofs, and very likely killed. When shooting in these vast pastures, I take care to give the herds a wide berth, and keep well away from them. Even then they will sometimes begin to move towards the dogs, in which case I put the setters or pointers, as the case may be, into the buggy as soon as possible, and drive off out of the sight of the herd. In shooting grouse in Illinois, Iowa, and the other prairie States, the sportsman should take water in his buggy or wagon for himself and his dogs. The prairies are very spacious, the water-courses wide apart, the droughts sometimes .long and severe. If he thinks to find water in natural places for himself and his dogs, which need it oftener and more than ho, they will be very thirsty before he reaches any. If he comes to a house at such times, he will find that water is the most scarce and precious thing about the place. The well is all but dry. The farmer's horses are on short allowance. His milch cows are stinted, and stand lowing round the empty trough at the well half the night long. The people sometimes, in very dry seasons, have to haul water from a distance, as their own wells become dry, and their cattleand horses must be provided for. In this state of affairs it cannot be expected that the people will furnish half a bucket of water for a stranger or two and the dogs. Therefore when you start out from house or camp, take in your buggy or wagon a five-gallon jug of water as a thing of prime necessity.

4

SECTION 4

CHAPTER IV.
LATE PINNATED-GROUSE SHOOTING.

In the preceding chapter I have described the places and times to seek the pinnated grouse in the earlier part of the shooting season, and pointed out the methods of hunting for them by means of which satisfactory success is most likely to be obtained. We now come to the latter part of the season, the months of October and November, with that of December; for the resolute and hardy sportsmen who care nothing for cold and wet may sometimes prefer a bag of winter grouse to one of duck or brant. In the month of October the prairies have become brown, and later on the corn will have been wilted by the early frosts, if it has not been already. Some of the best shooting of the year, to my mind the very best, is now before the sportsman; but it needs work, and young beginners will not find the grouse so easy to kill as they were in August and September. In the early part of the season the best shooting hours were early and late in the day. Now it is the reverse; the middle of the day is the proper time. When I first came to Illinois, the grouse in October and later were mostly found in the prairie-grass. There has now been a change in their habits, and they seem to like best to lie in corn. I suppose the reason was that as prairies were much broken up, and the quantity of land in corn rapidly increased, the grouse found out that the lying in the corn was excellent, and the habit was soon formed. In the corn there is a great plenty of various kinds of food. The ground is mellow and affords excellent dusting places. In the West wheat is often sowed while the corn is still standing, being put in with a cultivator-plough. These wheat-fields in the corn are favorite places with the grouse, and I have many a time killed eighteen or twenty in one such field. Also, when wheat is sowed out upon the prairie, grouse will go to those fields at early morning. When the sun gets high, they will go into the prairie-grass, round the edges of the young wheat, and lie there all the middle of the day. Then there is nice shooting. At four or five o'clock, towards evening, the birds will go out upon the young wheat-fields again. This is in clear weather. On cloudy days the grouse stayon the wheat, the bare places of the prairie, and on ploughed land all day, and it is of no use to go after them. You may just as well stay in your tent or house as go after grouse, for you cannot get near them. If there are quail in the neighborhood, you may have sport with them. In only one way can grouse be shot late in the fall in cloudy, overcast weather, and it is hardly worth while to employ that. You may drive up in a buggy, as we do in plover-shooting, and so get near enough, but it is more trouble than the game you will kill *is* worth, and I never do it. I may say here that those who go out shooting in the prairie States need to have a wagon or buggy with them. It may be done without, but the work is very severe. The prairies are very wide, and it is a good way from one favorable point to another. When I first went to Illinois, seventeen years ago, I used to start out in the morning, on foot, and shoot all day. I used no dog at all then, and had but a poor, light gun, which did but little execution, though I shot middling well. When I had got about seven or eight grouse, I used to hide them and mark the place, to be taken-up on my way back. With this gun I speak of and common powder I have often shot away a pound of the latter to get twenty-five or thirty birds. I followed, in those days, the example of other people, and used shot several sizes larger than was necessary or proper. At that date we used No. 1 or No. 2 in October and November, and I believe I was one of the first to discover that with No. 6, from a good gun, with a strong charge of powder, the biggest cock-grouse that ever flew could be brought to the bag. At the end of my day's shooting at that period I used to have to carry twenty-five or thirty grouse as well as the gun for four or five miles, sometimes further. This was no small matter.

The October shooting of grouse, good as that is, may be excelled, according to my notions, by that in November. They generally lie in the corn among the tumble-weed, so called from its growing up and rolling over so as to form snug cover; and they are especially fond of lying in the sod-corn, which is that grown upon the land the first crop after the prairie is broken up. This sod-corn does not grow up tall, as the corn on older-tilled land does. In November the blades of the corn are hanging down, wilted by the frost. The stalks are shrunk. The dogs canwork in it, and you can see to shoot in it. But it takes good shooting to make good bags. The birds are now at full growth and strength. They have in all probability flown the gauntlet of many guns, and the weaker ones have been thinned out of the packs. But on clear days they lie well to the dogs, and, being swift and strong on the wing, when they rise the sport afforded is capital. One of the best days I ever had was in November, near Farmer City, Champagne County, Illinois. I was accompanied by Mr. Nathan Doxie, of Geneseo, a keen sportsman and good shot. *A,t* that time he shot with a muzzle-loader, while I used a breech-loader. It was a clear, bright day, warm for the time of year. We beat the sod-corn, of which there was a great deal in the neighborhood, and, when the birds flew out into the adjoining prairie, we could mark them down. Our bag was a very heavy one. I killed fifty-seven grouse and Mr. Doxie knocked over eighteen, making seventy- five fine fat birds in all. Mr. Doxie said it was the first time he had ever been beaten in the field. There was another person shooting near us all day, but he did next to nothing, killing but five grouse, as I remember. I have shotwith many men in the month of November, and good shots too, but never one that I did not beat.

Three times in the course of my experience in field-shooting I have killed ten grouse with two barrels. Once in Menard County, near Salt Creek, late in November, I came upon a plank fence in a light snow-storm. It happened that there was a grapevine growing thickly over part of the fence, and, getting this between me and the birds, I secured a pretty close shot. They were scattered along the fence for a distance of about ten yards. With the first barrel 1 killed nine, and with the other one. Another time I got a shot at a lot near a fence, and killed ten with two barrels. And once in Logan County I got within shot of about twenty birds which were in short grass, and killed ten with both barrels. Such shots as these are very seldom to be got. A man may shoot half a lifetime and never meet with one. I have often, in the early part of the season, killed a grouse with each barrel out of a pack which rose near me, and then slipped in another cartridge, and killed a third. But this is only to be done when they are lazy and fly slowly, and it cannot be done then unlessthe shooter is very quick. Some men say that I am slow because I will not shoot until I have sighted the bird; but I think these sort of field- shots and my time-matches at pigeons are sufficient to prove the contrary. I believe I am as quick as anybody I ever met, but I will not fire at random, and I advise the reader never to do so. Late in the fall, when grouse get up a little wild, and fly swiftly, it takes good shooting and hard hitting to kill them. Sometimes in November, on a clear day and rather warm, they lie close, and get up one after the other after the first of the pack have gone. There are always some lying scattered from the body of the pack, and as one falls down, fluttering its wings, another will rise, sometimes two. On such occasions the immense superiority of the breechloader over the old sort of gun becomes manifest. I have been at such a time shooting with a man who used a muzzle-loader, and have actually stood in my tracks and shot six grouse while he was loading his gun. The grouse will sometimes lie so close on a clear day in November that they will remain hidden until you are within ten yards of them, and then get up with a tremendous whirr of wings. It is things of

this sort that sportsmen will be glad to know and what 1 state is drawn from experience solely

At the same season of the year, if the weather is cloudy and damp, the birds are so wild that you cannot get near them; and to try is to lose your time and labor for nothing. The Indian Summer is a good time for shooting grouse, and very pleasant for the sportsman. The sun has not the scorching power which you feel in August and the early part of September; but it is warm, the air soft and still, and not very hczy|rather like thin, white smoke scattered from a great distance. The birds feel comfortable in the dead grass of the prairie or among the sod-corn. They are fat and lazy, and hate to get up until compelled to do so. Any clear, warm day late in October or in November is just as good as an Indian Summer day. At this season it is useless to go out before the dew is off the grass; whereas in the earlier part of the shooting the more you get into the thick of it at early morning, the better for you. The prairies are handsome in the fall of the year, but not so beautiful as in the spring, when the grass is about six inches high and full of wild flowers. The weather is fine, the air pleasant and fragrant. Thecock-grouse which have flown out of the bottoms at early day arc heard booing on the knolls and ridges. Hawks of various kinds, large and small, are wheeling about overhead, and far away, high up in the distance, you may see the great eagle circling and sailing round about with motionless wings. But of all the sights I have seen on the prairies, the finest, the most striking and glorious, have been on bright, frosty mornings in December, or later on in the winter sometimes. On such a morning, while the frost still hangs on the grass, the prairie looks like a wide sea covered with sprays of diamonds. The most beautiful sight I ever saw in my life was on a prairie at Oliver's Grove, near Chatsworth, Iroquois County, Illinois. We went in the night to Chatsworth, where there was no house then, intending to hunt turkeys at Oliver's Grove at early morning. As there was no house at Chatsworth Station, we stayed in the car till daylight. It was a bright, clear morning in December, and the sun, just risen, lit up all the prairie with its horizontal, glancing rays. Every blade of grass on the prairie, every tree in distant grove, glistened and sparkled like diamonds in strong light. Away in the distance, five hundred yards out upon the prairie, there stood twodeer, motionless and beautiful we might almost have thought lifeless, they looked so strange in that wonderful scene; only we could see the breath streaming from their nostrils into the cold, frosty air. For dazzling radiance and strange beauty, I never before saw such a prospect, and may perhaps never see quite the like again. After a while the deer walked leisurely off into the long grass and brush near the slough to lie down in cover. The game we came for were not to be found, and when we discovered this we turned to leave. I said to my partner, " We have been disappointed in our hunt, but in coming on it we got a glorious and beautiful sightlone not to be forgotten as long as we may live."

He was a very practical sort of man, and replied, " I had a good deal sooner have got a dozen fat turkeys."

On our way back to Onarga across country we had to walk fourteen miles. There were many buckwheat-stubble patches along the prairie in our way, and we took them on our road to walk up the grouse. Ve did not diverge to the right or left to follow those which went away, but, keeping right ahead, got about twenty brace by the time we reached Onarga. Although there were no

turkeys about Oliver's Grove just then, it was a good place for them, and from what I saw there must have been lots of deer in the neighborhood. In regard to grouse-shooting late in the fall of the year, there is one thing which should be particularly observed. It is the necessity of silence. There should be very little or no talk indulged in between those who are on the beat. In the earlier part of the season it does not much matter what talk there is, though I am one of those who can stand a good deal of silence, when hunting, at any time; but late in the fall talking makes the grouse get up out of distance. They will rise at the sound of the human voice at that season of the year sooner than they will at the crack of the gun. If two men go along talking and gabbling, as I have seen and heard them do, the grouse will nearly all rise out of shot, while they would have lain long enough to have afforded many fair shots if silence had been preserved. In order not to be obliged to talk and call to my dogs at such times, I have them broken to hunt to the whistle and the motion of the hand. I have had some dogs that would hunt all day and never make it necessary to speak to them. I have been out with men who would talk in spite of remonstrancesagainst it. Either they did not believe it would scare up the birds, or it was not in their power to keep silent for half an hour at a time. There are, indeed, some .people who never seem to be silent except when asleep, and very likely not then if dreams come over them. On these talking occasions late in the fall I have always noticed that we got very few grouse. Sometimes when I have believed a pack of grouse to be all up, I have spoken a word or two to one of the dogs, when two or three more birds have risen right away. Another thing to be noted is this: when you are shooting grouse late in the fall, and the dog brings in a wounded one which flutters his wings, all the others within hearing will get up. That sound sets them on the wing as a man's voice does, when they lie close at the loud report of the gun. I am not able to explain why this is, but so it is. There are many facts in nature in regard to the habits of game which the sportsman must accept, though he cannot arrive at the reason of them.

At one time in Illinois there was a difference as to the period at which grouse-shooting should cease. It was left to the counties. In Logan County and some others it was fixed for the firstof January. In other counties where the grouse abounded to the degree that the farmers thought they consumed too much of the crop, there was no close-time in January, February, and March. I do not think grouse ever do any appreciable damage to the crops. What grain they eat would be otherwise wasted. They may, however, do some little harm by consuming seed-wheat just after the sowing. They bite off and eat the blades of young wheat, but that often does more good than harm, and farmers sometimes turn calves into young wheat-fields to feed it off. The biting off done by grouse in the earlier stages has a tendency to make it stool well, I think. It is certain that the pinnated grouse does the farmer good by consuming grasshoppers and other insects which are troublesome and destructive. The law of Illinois in regard to shooting grouse is now uniform all over the State. The shooting ceases on the fifteenth day of January. Thus the shooting lasts five months. I am in favor of lopping off fifteen days at the commencement, making it September 1 instead of August 15 and another fifteen days at the end, making it cease on the first of January. It would then last four months. But the duration of the shooting-time is not of somuch importance as many people think. More are taken by trapping late in the season. To see the huge loads of grouse sent by railway to Chicago and on for the Eastern market, one would be at first inclined to suppose that the species must soon be extirpated; but this is an error. With good breeding-places and a fine spring the number of grouse produced is incalculable. No amount of fair shooting makes much impression on game in a good game country. In places where the game is sparse, as it appears to me to be in the Atlantic and Eastern States, save water-fowl on the sea-board, many guns may shoot so close that the proper head for a breeding-stock will not be left. It is altogether different with us. I went once to Christian County, Illinois, and shot round about the little town of Assumption from February 1 to May 20, the latter part of the time being on snipe. The game of all sorts was amazingly abundant. There was a great plenty of grouse and quail, and the number of ducks and geese was almost past belief. It is a varied sort of country with a good deal of low, wet ground, much prairie and much corn-land, *and* a great deal of hazel-brush along the creeks and on the edges of the groves of timber. It is a splendid country forgame. I killed six thousand head of all sorts while there|the most part, of course, being duck, snipe, and golden plover. The grouse were extremely abundant in the spring about there. At early morning the cock-grouse could be heard booming all over, like the constant lowing of an immense herd of cattle distributed in a great pasture. It is hardly necessary to say that the booming of the grouse is not ike the lowing of bullocks; what 1 mean is that the booming on every side pervaded the space all around. Christian County is about thirty miles southeast of Springfield, and is on the Illinois Central Railroad. At this time I hold the best place for sport of all sorts in the field to be in the tier of counties which includes Ford, Piatt, McLean, and Champagne Counties, as well as Christian County. Late in the fall, however, good grouse- shooting is to be met with all over the State, unless it be down southwest in Egypt, where there is but little prairie-land. As I have stated, great numbers of grouse are bred in the wide prairies which are still unbroken, and late in the fell these grouse pack and distribute themselves over the other parts of the State in vast numbers, feeding in corn-fields and wheat, oat, and buckwheat stubbles. Where I live the grouse are nearly asabundant in the latter part of the fall now as they were seventeen years ago. Perhaps I might say quite as abundant; but there is not anything like as many young grouse to be found in that neighborhood in August and September as there used to be. As long as the breeding-places remain it is safe to conclude that there will never be a scarcity of grouse in Illinois and the other prairie States. But though they are nearly as numerous, they are more difficult to kill than formerly. The young birds find the great corn-fields a place of safe refuge; and when the packs come in from the great prairies late in the fall, they are wild and swift. To get good sport the observations I have made as to weather, the best hours of the day at the different seasons, and so on, should be carefully heeded. The burning of pieces of prairie late in the spring should be avoided, and it can easily be done. Let the grass be burnt the preceding fall, or, which is perhaps still more desirable, *early* in the spring. In the latter case the grass would have sprung up in places high enough to hold the nests before the hen-birds wanted to form them, besides which there are always many places untouched by the fire, and these spots would be chosen by the grouse to make their nests in. Byleaving the grass unburnt through the winter the birds would be afforded a protection in that season against their enemies|the various sorts of hawks, which are very numerous in the prairie States. The great source of mischief is the burning of the grass after the nests are made. I hope the farmers will follow my suggestions on this point. They are commonly ready to oblige sportsmen, and the latter should avoid anything which may cause annoyance while in pursuit of game.

SECTION 5

CHAPTER V.
QUAIL-SHOOTING IN THE WEST.

The beautiful little game-bird of which I am now about to write is well known in almost all parts of the country. It is a welcome visitor about the homesteads of the farmer in the winter season, and makes pleasant the fields and brakes in spring and summer. Quail are now very abundant in the Western States, much more so, I believe, than in those of the Atlantic seaboard, although they are found in considerable numbers in New York, New Jersey, Pennsylvania, Maryland, and Virginia. They are much more numerous now in Illinois and the other prairie States than they were formerly. I think the cul- .tivation of the land and the growth of Osage orange hedges have brought about the increase. The hedges furnish excellent nesting-places, and are also of great use to the quail as places of refuge and security when pursued by hawks. The latter are very hard on quail. Quail like the neighborhood of cultivated land, and where theyare not much shot at they will get so tame as to come right up to the house and barn. They used to have a very hard time of it in Illinois in severe winters. There was no protection from hawks, by which they were constantly harried and destroyed; and there being next to no cover, they used to be frozen to death in bevies. When the snow melted, the skeletons and feathers would be found in groups of eight or ten. The hedges now afford very great protection in severe weather, and preserve the lives of thousands which would otherwise certainly perish of cold and starvation in their absence. They break the force of the wind, and furnish snug-lying places for the birds in hard weather. In soft snow quail commonly manage to do very well in the open. When pursued by hawks at such times, they dart under the snow, and lie safely hid from their voracious enemies. I have seen them do this hundreds of times, and have rejoiced at their escape from the talons of the swift and persevering foe. In two or three instances I have walked up and caught the quail which had thus dashed into the yielding snow by hand. The quail is a very interesting bird about breeding-time, and the soft, whistling note of the cock isone of the plcasantest things that strike the ear in the fields in spring-time. They pair with us about the first of May. I have seen them together in bevies as late as, or later than, the middle of April. They build their nests along the hedges and near old fences overgrown with brush and brambles. They resort but little to the groves of timber for breeding purposes, avoiding them, I think, on account of egg-sucking vermin, such as skunks and crows. Crows are bold, cunning, and persistent robbers of the nests of other birds. Minks catch the old hens on the nest, and raccoons do the same. But the most destructive and inveterate enemy the quail has is the little hawk, called with us the quail-hawk. This little bird of prey is but a trifle larger than a quail himself, but it is very fierce and strong, swift on the wing, and darts upon its prey with electric speed. The nest of the quail is round, nicely constructed of small twigs, and lined with dead grass. I have seen statements to the effect that they are covered over on the top. I have found hundreds of them, and never saw one that was. The hen lays from twelve to fifteen eggs, but two hens sometimes lay in one nest, and I have seen one in which there were no less than thirty eggs. The hen-

quail does not seem to be very particular at times about having a nest of her own. I have known them to lay in the nests of pinnated grouse, and in those of barn-door fowl which had made their nests in hedges or bunches in weeds in fence-corners. It is always easy to learn when quail are breeding in the neighborhood, for at such times as the hen is laying or sitting the cock perches on a fence, a stump, or an old corn.stock, and whistles for joy. The note seems to express great satisfaction and delight. The young quail are no sooner hatched than they are active and ready to follow their mother. The latter is very watchful, attentive, and devoted, ready to risk her own life to afford a chance of safety to her offspring. If a man or a dog approaches the whereabouts of her young brood, the mother simulates lameness, and flutters about as if in a crippled condition, to lead the intruder another way. The early broods come off about the middle of June, when, the spring being forward, the birds have paired early. I saw young quail and young grouse this year myself in the middle of June. It is my impression that when the season is early and other circumstances favorable, the hen-quail raises two broods. I have often seen early broods under the care of thecock, and I think the hen was then sitting again. Furthermore, later in the year bevies of quail will be found in which there are manifestly birds of two sizes besides the old ones. These bevies must be made up of young quail of different ages. ' I am not certain as to the hen bringing forth a second brood while the first is under the care of the cock, but I state the facts I have seen for what they are worth. There is nothing improbable, to my mind, in the raising of two broods a year. The hen-quail is very prolific of eggs; food is abundant and stimulating at the breeding season; the weather is commonly steadily fine when the first brood is brought off, and the cock-bird is abundantly able to take care of it. In the State of Illinois quail-shooting begins on the first of October. I think the law ought to be changed so that it should not commence before the fifteenth of October. On the first of October some birds are full grown, but it is otherwise with the great majority of the young birds. Quail are a little slower in growth than pinnated grouse, and it is not before the fifteenth of October that most of the birds are large, strong, and swift of wing. In Ohio, Indiana, Michigan, Minnesota, Wisconsin, and other

wheat-growing States, there is very fine quail- shooting sooner in the season than there is in Illinois. With us the best shooting cannot be enjoyed until late in the fall. Before that time the immense corn-fields enable the quail to get the best of the sportsman. As soon as a bevy is flushed away it goes for the corn, which is thick, broad in the blade, and very high. I stand six feet in height, and I have seen stalks of Illinois corn so tall that I could but just reach the lowest ears upon them. There is no making headway and filling the bag in such fields as these; and the moment the quail are flushed on the wheat and oat stubbles away they go for the corn. You may give them up as soon as they reach this tall, thick, and dense cover. If you make an attempt at them in it, they will not rise above the tops, so that you cannot see to shoot; besides which, the thickest spread of the broad blades is just about as high as your head, and above it. It is not until good, sharp frosts have wellwilted the blades and caused them to hang down lifeless along the stalk that there is a good chance at the quail in such places. As long as the leaves wave crisp in the autumn wind the quail may defy the shooter. Thereforethe best of the shooting is in November and December. You must be up by dawn of day, and scatter the hoar frost or the sparkling dew as you go to your chosen grounds. In a country where there are many stubbles, many corn-fields,' and much hazel-brush the quail delight, and there, on such a morning, as soon as the sun has risen over the swells of the prairies to the eastward, they will be found in abundance. They roost along the margins of sloughs in long grass, in stubbles where the rag-weed is thick and strong, in patches of brush, and along hedge-rows. Where there are corn-fields along the margin of sloughs, the quail are fond of roosting in the edges of the corn. As soon as the sun touches the frost on the corn and grass and the weeds of the overgrown stubbles, the quail begin to run from their roost- ing-places. At the early hours, when they are first on the move, is the best time for the dogs to find them, as the scent is thAi very good. When they are really plentiful, they may be easily found in any weather, but most easily on a fine, olear day, early in the crisp, cool air of the bright, frosty morning. When a bevy is flushed in such weather as this, they scatter at once, and when they pitch down they lie there hid under the first bunch ofgrass or weed or any other bit of cover they can find for the purpose of concealment. With good dogs you can then take them one after the other. When a bevy has been flushed, and the birds have scattered about and pitched down in this way, I have often killed from six to ten before picking any up. I was once shooting in Mason County, Illinois, late in the fall, and flushed a very large bevy of quail from a wheat-stubble. They scattered and flew over into a piece of prairie-grass, where they pitched down. I knew they would lie very close, and so they did. They got up one and two at a time, and out of the bevy I accounted there and then for seven brace and a half. Quail pack late in the fall, and in Mason County at that time there were bevies of thirty or forty in number. In damp or wet weather quail act in a different manner when flushed and scattered. At such times, instead of lying where they pitch down, they run a long distance. And then when the dog has winded them, and is about to point, or has pointed, they start and run on again. Under such circumstances it is difficult to make a good bag. It was mainly in such weather that the netting of quail was carried on. This bad practice is now unlawful. I saw great numbers caught withnets in Missouri. Whole bevies were taken at one fell swoop, the quail being driven into the wings of the net by men on horseback. It is a very good thing that this destructive practice has been prohibited by law, and is now wholly done away with. As long as it was lawful the farmers on whose land it was practised did not like to interfere; but now they do interfere, and netting in Illinois and Missouri has practically ceased and corne to an end. When it was lawful, two netters were harder on the quail than about two hundred shooters, although at that time some of the latter who were apt to miss a bird on the wing would fire at bevies of quail on the ground. This is not a practice to be followed. I have taken two or three raking shots at grouse sitting on fences in my time, but the opportunity was so rare and the temptation so great that it was just then irresistible.

The best quail-shooting I ever had was in the Sangamon River country, about where Salt Creek falls into it. There is upon Salt Creek and the Sangamon a great deal of bottom-land with much hazel-brush and considerable timber. There are also plenty of corn-fields. The shooting there is much varied. There are vast numbers of quail, agreat many grouse, and at the right times snipe and duck are to be Ibund in amazing numbers. When I used to go out in that neighborhood for the purpose of shooting, quail especially, I used to get from twenty to thirty brace a day for many days in succession. Varied shooting, however, is more satisfactory sport to me, and 1 used to make very heavy bags of grouse, quail, and some duck lmallards and teal. It is a great place for mallards; some of them stop all summer and breed there, and some stop all winter, for there are parts of the river which hardly ever freeze over. Quail are more abundant about there now than they were at the time I speak of, and there are quite as many grouse; but they are both more difficult to kill than they used to be in the earlier part of the season. The corn-fields have increased so that they are now many and vast, and this serves as a defence for the birds. There are more quail in that country this year than there ever were before. There are now, however, plenty of quail all over Illinois, Iowa, and Missouri. In the southwest of Illinois, the region called Egypt, there is a great deal of brush interspersed with prairie, farm-lands, and groves of timber, and there quail may be found in great abundance. Butgrouse are not as plentiful there as in the interior counties of the State.

Some people think the quail a hard bird to shoot, but it is not. It flies swift but straight, and is commonly missed by reason of the shooter being too much in a hurry where it is not brought to bag. Because the flight of the bird when flushed is rapid, men think it necessary to shoot very quick, and pull the trigger without sighting the mark truly. This is an error to which three out of four misses are owing. Let the bird be well sighted along the rib before the trigger is pulled, and, no matter how fast he goes, the shot will overtake and stop him. Quail will not carry off a great many shot. There is no necessity for hurry in shooting, and this will be made manifest to sportsmen if they will sometimes step the ground from where they fired to the dead bird. They will find that in nine cases out of ten it was not as far off as they believed it to be when they fired at it. Many of those thought to be as much as forty yards off when the trigger was pulled will be found dead at thirty yards, and some at five-and-twenty. This shows, that there is commonly plenty of time to get well on the bird before shooting, instead of blazing away on theinstant at random. I have shot thousands on thousands myself, and know that my misses were commonly caused by being in too much of a hurry to fire. When I have missed with the first and killed with the second barrel, I have considered it a plain proof that I ought to have let another second elapse before firing the first barrel; for if a bird, flying in the open straight away, or quartering, is well sighted with a good gun properly charged, it is next kin to a miracle for it to escape. After good experience I resolved to take -more time in quail-shooting, and I have found the practice answer. I can now kill nearly every quail I shoot at within fair distance. Quail generally lie close to the dog when they will lie at all well, and do not get up until the shooter is near them. The experience of sportsmen will confirm this, and it will show that there is no reason whatever for shooting in a hurried manner, but very strong reasons for guarding against it. By taking time you not only get the bird well sighted, but the extra distance it has gone gives the shot so much more chance to spread, and thus increases the chance to kill.

A few years ago, after the close of the war, 1 went, in the middle of January, on a shootingexcursion to Lynn County, Missouri. I hunted on Shoal Creek, in the neighborhood of Cameron, a place about fifty miles east of St. Joseph, on the Missouri River. It was a good place for game. There were quail, pinnated grouse, some ruffed grouse, turkeys and deer in large numbers. I killed many turkeys and a few deer; but of these I shall give some account further on, under the proper heads. The country is wild and broken, with much brush and timber, and abounds in gullies, deep hollows, and steep ravines. The bevies, when flushed, would frequently fly for the thickets and gullies, and then it was difficult shooting. Sometimes, however, they would scatter and drop in the grass of the pieces of prairie, and then I had beautiful sport, killing from twenty to thirty brace a day. The pinnated grouse were not numerous about there, but the ruffed grouse were in fair numbers for them. Iowa is a good State for quail. There are more groves of timber and more brush there than in Illinois, but the latter is much the best State for pinnated grouse, and the growing up of the Osage orange hedges has supplied in many parts the want of brush, and thus increased the head of quail. When flushed in the open, the birds veryoften go for the hedges, and then a great deal may be done with a gun on each side of the hedge while the dogs are beating it. One man cannot do much with the quail when they take this refuge. Some of these hedges are eight or ten feet high; others have been so trimmed as to be four feet through and thick of growth. With a man on each side of the hedge there is very pretty shooting. If you are out without a companion, and the quail take to the hedges, you may trust one side to an old, well-trained dog, and take the other yourself. Always send the dog to the lee side. If you have a companion, and he leaves to you the choice of sides, as most men will do, not knowing that it makes any difference, always take the windward side.

By so doing you will get three or four shots to your companion's one when the wind is blowing athwart, Ct nearly athwart, the hedge. The reason is very simple, though seldom thought of. The dog to leeward winds the quail in the hedge, and, as a matter of course, puts them out on, the windward side; while the scent is blown away from the dog on your side. I have been out with men who did not understand this, and they would say, " Captain, what the dl1 makes almost all the quail fly
f
out on your side of the hedge?" Half the success of sporting, outside of being a good shot, depends upon the knowledge of such things as this. There is another matter to be mentioned here. The best dogs in the world are sometimes unable to find and put up all the birds in a bevy of quail. I have often been out with men who had first-rate dogs, and have, to their amazement, given them absolute and irrefragable proof of this fact. They have been not a little annoyed at first when they saw me put up quail which their dogs had been unable to find after the bevy was gone. But it was no fault of the dogs, nor were they unable to detect the quail because the latter withheld their scent, as some have argued they have power to do. I do not believe they possess any such power. It is not a question of no scent, but of too much. The bevy have been lying there and running all over the ground, so that it is covered and tainted with scent to such a degree that the noses of the dogs become full of it, and that is why they cannot find and put up one or two birds which lie close in their hiding-places and decline to move. I will now relate a notable instance of this sort of thing which occurred last fall. It was near Selma,

Alabama, in the neighborhood of which city I was shooting with a gentleman named Ellis and Mr. Jacobs, a gunsmith. On the day in question Mr. Jacobs did not take the field, and Mr. Ellis and I were alone. He had a brace of splendid setters, a black and a red. For one of the dogs he had paid two hundred and fifty dollars, and he would not have taken five hundred for the brace. They had fine noses and were splendid workers. In the course of our sport we found a bevy of quail in old grass at the edge of a bit of prairie which had once been ploughed up, and was now an old garden all overgrown with weeds and briers. The quail ran in the grass, but finally got up together. Mr. Ellis killed two and I killed two. A few went away, and were marked down at some distance. Mr. Ellis believed they were all gone. The dogs beat the ground thoroughly, and could find no more. I said that 1 believed there-might be more, upon which Mr. Ellis made his dogs try it again, and then confidently pronounced that there could not be another quail there. I said, " I still think there may be quail here and I will show you how to make them rise if there are any." With that I imitated the kind of whistling noise made by the old quail

when she has young ones. Up got one, and Mr. Ellis killed it; away went another, and I stopped it. Mr. Ellis was greatly astonished, and did not know what to make of it. I explained the matter, telling him that if the dogs had been taken off to another part of the field, and kept there long enough for the old scent to have exhaled from the ground and passed away, they would have found the two quail readily enough when brought back to the place. The ground was so saturated with scent that the dogs could not distinguish that of the remaining birds, and could not put them up without stumbling right on them. I have often seen the same thing happen with a close-lying lot of pinnated grouse in long prairie-grass. I do not believe in the theory advanced by some that quail or any other game-bird can withhold their scent so as to prevent a good dog from winding them when he comes near. I had fair sport in the South last fall, principally at quail, round the cotton-fields, but there seemed to be a scarcity of game. There was not one quail to a hundred which would have been found in good situations in Illinois. I was in Alabama, Louisiana, Mississippi, and Tennessee, and nowhere was game in what we should call fair plenty in the West. At Paris, Tennessee, they

held the erroneous opinion that a pigeon-shooter could not be a good field shot. They said they had a man who could beat any pigeon-shooter in the field. I told them to send for him, as I was willing to shoot against him for a hundred dollars, fifty shots each, to be taken alternately. They would not make the match. In Mississippi I shot with Mr. Galbraith. The birds were scarce and wild. There were more about Selma than any other place I was at. So far as my experience went, the shooting was nothing to .that which may be had in Ohio, Indiana, Illinois, Michigan, Iowa, Wisconsin, Minnesota, Kansas, Missouri, Nebraska, etc. There were as fine a lot of gentlemen in the South as I have ever met, and they were good shots and keen sportsmen.

CHAPTER VI.
RUFFED-GROUSE SHOOTING.

Hitherto *we* have been concerned with the sport to be had in pursuit of game-birds, pinnated grouse, and quail, which are found in the neighborhood of cultivated farms, and, as regards the latter, often in the immediate vicinity of the habitations of man. We now come to one whose favorite haunts are wild, solitary places not frequently intruded upon, and almost always lying remote from thickly- settled sections of country. The ruffed grouse is a very handsome bird, and in situations where it is seldom shot at it seems to take a sort of pride in exhibiting its beauty in a stately and graceful manner. It weighs about a pound and a half; is plump on the breast; and its flesh, white, juicy, and delicate, is delicious eating. It is usually half spoiled in city restaurants by splitting and broiling. It ought to be roasted and served with bread-sauce. The ruffed grouse is extensively distributed from east to west, but is nowhere found in any greatabundance. Its habits are not nearly so gregarious as those of the pinnated grouse, and no such multitudes are to be found anywhere of ruffed grouse as may often be met with of the former species in the great prairie States. The ruffed grouse is but seldom found in coveys, though sometimes a brood of full-grown birds are found still together in some lonely nook among the woodlands, or in a solitary, sheltered spot in severe winter weather. It is generally found singly or in pairs, and loves sylvan solitudes, steep hillsides, wooded dells, and the neighborhood of gullies and ravines. The rougher and more broken the country, the better the ruffed grouse like it, provided it ia well timbered with the trees and well covered with the shrubs upon whose buds the birds mainly feed. It is, however, often met with in the deep, heavily-timbered bottom-lands of the northwest part of Michigan. The buds of birch, beech, and laurel (so-called) are the favorite food of this bird in winter and spring. In summer it no doubt feeds largely on berries and insects. I do not think it ever visits the stubble-lands to pick up wheat and buckwheat, though there are some such bits of stubble in the very heart of the woods in which it is constantly but thinlyfound. In the New England States it is met with, and is sparsely distributed in New York and New Jersey. In some of the wild, half- mountainous tracts of New Jersey, where tho undergrowth consists largely of laurel, it is more abundant. It is also frequently met with in West Virginia. In Kentucky, Ohio, Indiana, Illinois, Missouri, and Iowa the ruffed grouse is also found; but so far as my knowledge and experience go, it is most abundant of all in some parts of Wisconsin and the northwest part of the lower peninsula of Michigan. It is said fhat the buds of the laurel and some of the berries upon which the ruffed grouse feed have a tendency to make the flesh poisonous. I cannot confirm the theory, though I have eaten many a grouse whose crop was full of the buds in question when drawn. In general appearance it has some resemblance to the pinnated grouse, but is a smaller bird, with a long, square tail, very full feathered, which it carries over thd fallen leaves and mossy sward among the timber with a conscious pride and a swelling, strutting gait in places where it is little disturbed. It is, in fact, a beautiful ornament to the romantic solitudes and deep, heavy woods which it inhabits.In places where it is seldom shot at, the bird, at the approach of man, instead of taking wing, often spreads its tail, ruffles up the feathers of the neck, and struts off with the proud air of the true cock of the woods. In the spring of the year, at the approach of breeding-time, and at other seasons just before stormy, rainy weather, the male bird drums at dawn of day. It may sometimes, too, be heard performing this singular feat in the night, and on a sultry afternoon when a thunder-storm is brewing. The drumming is usually made on an old log, and each male bird seems to have his favorite place for the joyous performance. He begins by lowering his wings as he walks to and fro on the log, then making some hard strokes at intervals, and finally so increasing the swiftness of the movement that the sound is like the rapid roll of a snare-drum muffled by a position in the depths of the woods. The sound is very deceptive as to the place of the birtl. He may be comparatively near, while his drumming really seems like muttered thunder a long way off. On the other hand, the hearer sometimes supposes the hidden drummer to be close at hand when he is at a very considerable distance. In wild situations, near lonely precipices, the beating of the ruffed grouse upon his log may remind one of Macdonald's phantom drummer, whose story was beautifully and forcibly told in verse by General William H. Lytle, who fell, covered with glory and renown, at Chickamauga:

" And still belated peasants tell
How, near that Alpine height,
They hear a drum roll loud and clear

On many a storm-vexed night.
This story of the olden time

With sad eyes they repeat,
And whisper by whose ghostly hands

The spirit-drum is beat."

I have often seen the tops of old logs divested of their mosses and worn smooth by the constant drumming of the cock ruffed grouse, and have stood within thirty yards and seen the bird perform the operation. Just before rain the grouse drum frequently, and the repetition of this sound from various quarters in the daytime is a pretty certain indication of the near approach of wet weather. The female builds in the Western States about the first of May. The nest is formed of leaves and dead grass, and is built ina secluded place at the root of a tree or stump, or by the side of an old, mossy log overgrown with blackberry briers. The hen lays from twelve to fifteen eggs, and when first hatched the chicks are the most beautiful, cunning, and alert little things that can be seen anywhere. The editor of this work had an excellent opportunity for observing them and their watchful, devoted mothers on one well-remembered occasion. Nearly thirty years ago he was upon an exploring expedition in the northwest part of the lower peninsula of Michigan. The country was then very thinly settled about there. A few men had with much labor hewn out little clearings in the heavy-timbered woods in places on the banks of rivers, but the great industry was logging in the pine-woods, splitting shingles, and fishing during the spring freshets, when the lowlands and wet prairies were literally covered with pickerel. The ridges were thickly timbered with beech and maple where not covered with pine, and the bottom-lands were clothed with gigantic oak, black-walnut, basswood, hickory, and butternut trees. It was a country watered by a network of rivers, which united to form the Saginaw, soon after which junction the latter fellinto the bay of the same name in Lake Huron. We started in canoes, well provided with provisions, arms, and ammunition, and paddled for the mouth of the Cass. It was in June, and the young flappers (wild ducks) were swarming in the rivers. Above the bend of the Cass we made our first camp. The region was then very wild. Deer abounded, and the wolves howled hideously around the camp at night. We treed two or three wild-cats, and shot them with rifles. We had no shot-guns. A baiid of Chip- pewa Indians were encamped near us. The men of the tribe lived by hunting and fishing with the spear. The women and girls made money by gathering cranberries in the marshes when the wild fruit was ripe. These Indians assured us that a few elk were still left in the great woods which here surrounded our party, and they said that in the fall there were lots of bears. It was just the hatching-time of the ruffed grouse, which we found numerous in the bottoms among the heavy timber. They had seldom been molested, and were not very shy, but rather bold and fearless. One day we cut down a butternut- tree, wanting it to make a temporary bridge across a creek, and, having lopped the top, wentto our tent to dinner. On our return we came upon a hen-grouse with a brood of young newly hatched. Uttering a cry, she scuffled and fluttered about at our feet with the most motherly courage and devotion, behaving as if she were wounded, in order to draw us oflf. But we had seen her young ones run under the leaves of the fallen butternut-tree, and caught two or three of them. They were beautiful downy little things, and watched us intently with their bright eyes. The mother, stimulated by alarm, remained near us while we held her young after the others had scuffled off, and we had the pleasure of placing the little things on the ground again, and seeing them hide in the cover. We walked away to a distance, and soon heard the mother calling her brood of little ones to the shelter of her protection. The yoraig are very quick and cunning at concealment. As soon as they hear the mother's warning cry they dart into cover, and, if there is no other at hand, they will seize a leaf with bill and feet, and turn over so that it may conceal them. While the party remained above the bend of the Cass river there came up a tremendous thunder-storm, followed by a cold wind from Lake Huron. Previous to the storm the cock ruffedgrouse could be heard drumming in all directions. It is a flat, alluvial country, much of the bottomland being overflowed early in spring, as all the -et prairies thereabouts are; but, nevertheless, these bottoms abounded with grouse in the breeding-season.

The ruffed grouse can seldom be relied upon to fill the game-bag alone; for the most part it is sparsely and thinly distributed over the regions it inhabits, though in some secluded spots where they have not been disturbed a good number may sometimes be killed in the fall before the broods have dispersed. It is as wild in disposition as any bird that flies. The young of the pinnated grouse may be brought up in confinement, but I do not think those of the ruffed grouse can be reared in the same way. I began to shoot ruffed grouse, when still a boy, in the neighborhood of Burnville, Albany County, New York, in company with a man named Paul Hochstosser. He was a hunter by calling, and a good one, well versed in the woodcraft of the region, and the best shot with the double-barrelled gun then in those parts. The first bird I ever killed was a ruffed grouse perched in a hemlock-tree. He was on an arm close to the trunk of the tree, bolt upright, withhis neck stretched up. This is their habit when they take to trees, and they are not easily distinguished from knots. 1 knew their habits, and had good eyes. That day I had played truant from school, and, taking my father's old firelock, I went out to hunt. The greater part of the day was gone before 1 got one of the birds I saw in a proper sitting position. However, there he was at last, and as I was too small to hold the musket out and take aim from the shoulder alone, I steadied it against the bole of another tree. Bang she went, and down came the grouse, but only winged. There was snow on the ground, and, boy- like, I dropped the old musket into it, and went for the wounded grouse. The ground was a steep hillside, the bird fluttered down it, and I went after, tumbling and rolling for as much as a hundred yards. But I secured it at last, and thinking it was glory enough for one day, as the saying is, I recovered the old musket and returned home. The truancy was condoned because of the bird. After that I hunted every time I could get a chance to do so. I soon got hold of a single-barrelled gun with a percussion-lock, and by perseverance for some time learned to shoot on the wing. Paul was a great woodcock-shooter, andwe sometimes shot in company. In going after ruffed grouse in those days we used to take a small spaniel dog, which would flush them out of the brush, and cause them totake to the trees. They are not easy to distinguish, as 1 said before, when on the tree, from their sitting upright close to the trunk, their plumage being somewhat the color of the bark. This habit must be remembered by the sportsman when he believes the bird is treed, but is unable to make him out. When several have taken to the same tree, shoot the one which sits lowest first, and the others will not take wing. If the upper one is shot, its fall starts the others off. More ruffed grouse are shot sitting than flying. It is a very hard bird to shoot on the wing|hard to hit and hard to kill. Other birds, when flushed in woodland, fly for the openings in the trees; the ruffed grouse, on the contrary, plunges right into the densest part of the thicket. The man who commonly kills the ruffed grouse he shoots at on the wing is fit to hold his own at any sort of shooting on the wing. The bird commonly rises in difficult ground with a whirr like the sudden roar of a waterfall, and goes away at electric pace for the thickest part of the brake. The birda were scarce in Albany County, New York. The most I ever killed in a day there was six. In Cook County, Illinois, 1 have killed fifteen in a day. In Missouri, on Shoal Creek, when I was hunting-turkeys, I found ruffed grouse in fair numbers, considering the nature and habits of the bird, and killed forty or fifty in the three weeks I stayed there. Of all the places I know, the ruffed grouse are most plentiful in the timber-lands of Wisconsin and Minnesota and the upper part of Michigan. But it is a bird of very secluded habits, and when settlements have become thick and much of the timber has been cleared off, it disappears. A well-watered timber country, with plenty of thick underbrush among rifts and gullies, is the place to look for it as a common rule, though they are also found in the great woods of heavy-timbered bottom-land. In looking for ruffed grouse especially I use No. 8 shot, and, if I found them while turkey-shooting, I changed the cartridge. I do not use spaniels now, but shoot ruffed grouse over setters. They will lie pretty well to the dogs sometimes, and where not shot at will sometimes strut off in front of him in plain sight. When shot at much and wild, the ruffed grouse must be pointed by the dog from a considerable distance. It will not let him get close, and as soon as the

setter moves a step forward the grouse springs up and goes away like a bullet for the thickest part of the cover. I have seen stories in print of ruffed grouse taking to water, of its being caught and let go, and then caught again. I do not believe one word of such things. The man who invented them can know but little of the nature and habits of this very wild bird. In the deep snows of winter the ruffed grouse roost under the snow. They dart at it with great speed, and make a sort of burrow beneath the surface. At other times they roost on the ground. When out coon-hunting at night, I have often put them up from their roosts on the ground. It has been maintained that they sometimes roost in trees; and as they certainly take to trees readily enough when flushed by a barking dog, and feed on the buds of trees, it seems reasonable to believe that they may sometimes roost in them. On the other hand, many men of experience declare that they *never* roost in trees. I have often seen them in -trees very early in the morning, but it was out at the ends of the branches, feeding on the young buds. I will not positively affirm that the ruffed grouse never roosts in trees, but I think it never does so when it can help it. In very severe weather,when the crust upon the snow is too strong to be pierced, the bird may seek shelter under the thicjc boughs of pines, and close to the trunk on the leeward side. It can stand a great deal of cold, and, unlike some other birds, can always find its food|the buds and tender twigs of trees and shrubs|in the hardest weather. The sportsman who goes into the places the ruffed grouse frequents will see some of the most picturesque scenes and romantic landscapes that the country affords. Hills and ravines, secluded woodland dells, the foliage rich and ripe with the deep tints of autumn, will meet his eye, while the music pf mpuntain-brooks and .the roar of waterfalls will fill his ears.

6

SECTION 6

CHAPTER VII.
SHOOTING THE WOODCOCK.
In the estimation of sportsmen in this country, as well as in Europe, the woodcock is regarded as one of the very highest game-birds. To make a good bag of woodcock is a feat to be proud of. The bird is generally scarce, even on the best ground, and in its most favorite haunts it is difficult to find and kill, and is one of the richest morsels on the table that the woods and fields supply. The woodcock of America slightly differs from that of Europe in size and markings, but the variations are of no moment to the sportsman. Upon this continent the woodcock winters in the Southern States, and in regions still further south, and comes north in spring, remaining till the ground freezes late in .the fall. The bird breeds in Canada and Nova Scotia, as well as in northern and middle States of the Union, East and West; and it sometimes rears two broods in a season. This is not, however, commonly

the case, but it is certain that when the old birds have lost their nests or their young through floods in the breeding-time, they rear a late brood. The woodcock arrives north in March, and generally builds in April. Much depends, however, upon the earliness or lateness of the spring, which sometimes varies nearly a month. Its nest has been found in March in very early situations, but it is believed that in such cases they were those of old birds which had passed a mild winter in some chosen, sheltered spot, and never gone south at all. It is reasonable that after having made its migration from the far south to the latitude of New York, Illinois, Michigan, and Canada, the birds would require some weeks for restoration before laying their eggs. The nest is made on the ground, in a piece of woods or brushy swamp, and is composed of grass and leaves. The hen lays four, sometimes five eggs, and the young run as soon as hatched; the little ones are active and rather cunning at hiding, though not to such an extent as the chicks of the ruffed grouse. The woodcock displays the same care and manifests as much devotion to her young as the ruffed grouse, and employs the same expedient of simulating lameness to draw off an intruder from their neighborhood. The hen-woodcock is a tame bird when sitting, and will not leave her nest for any light reason. When I was a boy, they used to build in a swamp on my father's farm in Albany County, New York, where I have more than once crawled up and caught the old bird in my hand, and released her after looking at her eggs. This would not induce her to forsake her nest, and in this she differs from some other wild birds. Wild ducks are not easily driven from their nests, and, after being disturbed once or twice, will still return again. The English pheasant, if once flushed directly off her eggs, always forsakes them. I never saw more than five eggs in a woodcock's nest, and usually there are but four. It has been stated that a woodcock's nest, with eight full-fledged young ones, was found on the banks of Loch Lomond, in Scotland. I believe these were the young of some other bird, if eight were found, for the story is almost absurd on its face. Young woodcocks, full-fledged, are never found in a nest. The young, when first hatched, might be, but they are then covered with dowle, and not with feathers. The woodcock has been kept in confinement, and proved

itself to be a voracious feeder. It Vas no small trouble to keep it supplied with worms. It bored in to the earth given to it, and was always ready for food. The digestion of the woodcock is very rapid. This accounts for the fact that birds which arrive poor speedily get condition in good ground.

For the procurement of its food, for which it bores in soft, moist ground, fat, loamy soils, and rich vegetable mould, it has a long, slender bill, very sensitive, and a long, prehensile tongue with barbs on the end. The young grow rapidly where the lying is good and the food plentiful. In favorable seasons they have attained their growth by tho fourth of July, when the shooting commences. But in some places, in some years, they are not above two-thirds grown at that date. I saw woodcock at Boston this year in the middle of July not two-thirds grown, and it was a pity they had been shot. After the broods have once dispersed, the woodcock is a solitary bird. It is true that a number of them may sometimes be found in the same swale, " cripple," or piece of woodland, but that is because the lying of the place suits them, and the boring is good, worms and the larvse of insects

being abundant in the soil. The woodcock does not frequent sandy, thirsty soils, nor gravelly ground, nor sour, wet meadows. It wants warmth and richness, as well as plenty of moisture. The bird is nocturnal in its habits, and its great eye, placed far backwards and upwards in its large head, enables it to see by night and in the gloom of the thick coverts in which it lies by day. It never flies by day, unless disturbed, and seldom feeds in the daytime, unless it be on rare occasions in the thick shade of some moist and closely- overgrown spot in its cover. Late in the evening, when it is nearly dark, the woodcock leave the cover, and betake themselves to wet, rich places to bore for their food. It used to be a popular notion that woodcock and snipe ate nothing, and lived merely by what was called suction; whereas they are both voracious feeders and like the richest quality of food|namely, the plump worms and insects to be found in fat soils. After industriously spending the night in finding food to satisfy his enormous appetite, the woodcock returns just before dawn of day to the thick brake or close overgrown " cripple," in which he lies while the daylight lasts. Where there is good lying and good feeding ground, woodcock may befound in the season, and in spots where one bird has been shot it is common for another to take its place in a day or two. Where such birds come from, and why they did not come before the place was tenantless, is not known. Although in some sort methodical in its ways and habits, the woodcock often seems to be erratic in its comings and goings to and from certain localities. Some days the birds will be found plentiful, for them, in certain ground. On another day, without any obvious reason for their absence, not one can be puf up in the same piece. The weather or some other cause unknown has induced them to make a local change, and this has sometimes been magnified, I think, into a second migration or a permanent removal to the uplands and bluffs. I do not believe that there is any second migration northwards of the woodcock after breeding-time; nor do I believe that the birds go to the uplands and bluffs, and stay there until the beginning of October. It is not true that no woodcock are to be found in their usual haunts in September. I have found and shot them myself in that month in fair numbers. It is true that there arc not as many as there were in July, and for the verygood reason that vast numbers have been shot, while those which are left have become moro wild and wary. Another reason for the seeming absence of birds, except hero and there, is simply this: with us, grouse-shooting in the latter part of August and September is so much easier, and affords so much greater chance of success, that very few go after woodcock in those months, and the birds have it all to themselves in woody swales, tangled thickets, and the islands overgrown with the willow and the alder, until October brings down the great division of birds bred to the northward of the United States.

Early in the season and during the hot weather the woodcock is a lazy bird, and seems to labor in its flight. It is not, however, easy to kill on that account, for when it rises, often very close to you, it goes up among the thick foliage, right on end, as it were, to the top of the cover, and then, after flying horizontally for about twenty yards, it suddenly flops clown again. When it does this after being shot at, men often think they have killed it, while in truth not a feather has been touched. The thickness of the covert in full leaf prevents the shooter from having anything but a glimpse of the bird, and he mustmake a snap-shot at where intuition tells him the woodcock ought to be. Besides this difficulty, the upward flight is calculated to distract the aim, even when the bird is not absolutely concealed by the density of the foliage. Commonly it is flip-flap of the wing, and the woodcock has gone away, often not seen by the sportsman at all. In some places it is practicable to send the dog in to beat the thicket while you remain on the edge to shoot as the cock fly. Where the brush is short this may be done, and, if there are many birds, the sport will be good. Three years ago I had some nice shooting by following this method on Rock River,

Illinois. When the cover is large, and the timber and saplings are twenty feet high, the above-mentioned plan will not work. You must go in then with the dogs, and take your chance of snap-shots. Later in the year the woodcock is sometimes found in more open- pieces of timber|that is, in places where the underbrush is not so very thick. But it is still a pretty hard bird to shoot, for now it flies like a bullet, and zigzags and twists about among the close-standing stems, going for an opening through which to make a straight flight. The woodcock flushed in cover always goes for anopening; the ruffed grouse never does, but sets sail for the closest and densest part. Now, when the woodcock is going swift and twisting among the stems of the saplings, he is very easy *to miss,* and sportsmen who make good bags of cock in the prime of the fall season have a right to be proud of their exploits. This sort of shooting is much more pleasant than that to be followed in the tangled " cripples" of New Jersey, all overgrown with cat-briers and thick brush, with no good footing where you are, and no possibility of knowing where you will be next. In Albany County, New York, wo used to use cooking-spaniels when woodcock-shooting. I have had none of that breed in the West, and now employ setters. They are bolder and better in forcing their way in rough places than pointers. The thin skins of the latter get all cut and torn, and their feet give out. But the best dogs I have ever had for general sport, take one sort of shooting with another, have been cross-bred between the setter and the pointer. For work these beat *any* purebred dog I ever owned, and, I may add, ever saw. But concerning this I shall treat further on. A great many woodcock may be found about Lockport, Illinois, forty miles southwest of Chicago, but the brush is so thick in the swamps in summer and early fall that the shooting is difficult. There are a few on the Sangamon, but only a few. On the bottoms and islands of the upper Mississippi- River, right down to St. Louis, many woodcock may be found. The bottoms and islands are rich alluvial mould, and the woodcock finds himself well placed in them for cover, for food and breeding-places. The brush commonly grows down to the water's edge, and old logs lie among the bushes. The woodcock also frequents the thickets on the edges of the bayous and sloughs, and, when the bottoms have been overflowed, the birds use them as soon as the water has receded. During the floods they shift their places, and lie further from the rivers, but in the same sort of ground as before. In New York they were sometimes found in wet corn-fields adjacent to cover, but I do not think they ever are in the West. On the Illinois River, about Pekin, Peoria, and Havana, there is fair woodcock-shooting; but the bird is scarce everywhere in the West, compared with other sorts of game. Indeed, the woodcock is not only relatively scarce in the West, but, as I thir.lt, absolutely scarcer than in the Atlantic States. Thereis not in the prairie States so much of the sort of ground the woodcock likes as there is further east. I do, indeed, know of plenty of ground in Central Illinois which one would think just suitable for woodcock, but, owing to some reason which I have never been able to discover, the birds are not found there. A stray one or two may be picked up occasionally, but they are never there in any number. I suppose it to be owing to some peculiarity in the soil. These neighborhoods have much of the right kind of food, and snipe abound near them; but for some reason the woodcock does not like them. About the middle of October there is a great increase in the number of woodcock in the bottoms and islands of the Mississippi and Illinois rivers. Flights of those bred

further north then arrive, and they stay until driven away by sharp frosts. When they first arrive from the North, the leaves are still thick, but the white frosts, which are quite insufficient to freeze the ground and drive the woodcock south, wilt the leaves, and then the shooting is pleasant and good. Generally speaking, the woodcock remain well along through November, and some seasons they have not all' gone by the 1st of December. They like the
    neighborhood of little streams which trickle through brush and among timber. The most T ever killed in a day was fifteen couple. I have heard men boast of having killed fifty couple in a day; but if they did it, the birds must have been vastly more abundant than I ever saw them anywhere. The woodcock is easily killed when you can get an open shot; but that is rather seldom, except at the last of the season and in such small patches of short brush as I mentioned above. A woodcock, when winged, does not run off as quail do. The birds have tw sorts of flight In one it goes laboring and slow, just over the tops of the branches, to which height it has risen almost perpendicularly, and then it soon flops down again. Its other mode of flight is swiftly away among the stems of the trees, darting here and there until it has found its opening, along which it goes like a bullet. 1 was told in the South that it is very plentiful along the edges of the bayous in the winter there. The negroes go out by night in boats with torches, and, paddling along, the woodcock on the muddy margin are knocked down with sticks. I heard of this, but never saw it, and merely tell the tale as it was told to me.

7

SECTION 7

CHAPTER VIII.
  THE SNIPE AND SNIPE-SHOOTING.
  This well-known and excellent Kttle bird of passage is to be found all over the country, in suitable ground, at the times of the spring and fall migrations. It winters about the wet rice- . fields of the Southern States, and comes north in the spring, going to its breeding-grounds, which are mainly in higher latitudes than the United States. It is true that a few remain all summer in the Eastern States, and also in those to the westward, and rear broods of young; but by far the larger number continue towards the north, pausing about a month in the middle latitudes. It does not breed south of Virginia. In Kentucky, Indiana, and Michigan some snipe are bred in the sedges of the wet prairies and about the edges of the wild rice-swamps. In Illinois a few nests are made about the Calumet, and some in the great Winnebago Swamp, which is part pool, and a great deal of high grass marsh. About Co- lurnbus, Kentucky, the first flights of spring snipearrive on the river-bottoms by the first of March in an early spring, but much depends upon the forwardness of the season and the state of the weather. The snipe need not be looked for until the frost is quite out of the ground, no matter how genial and pleasant the days may be. The reason seems to be plain. As long as there is frost in the ground the worms and larvas of insects upon which snipe feed

are underneath the frozen strata, and cannot be found in the soft mud of the surface. In Illinois and Northern Indiana the frost holds in the ground much longer than in Southern Kentucky. It penetrates a good deal deeper, and the spring is more backward than in the last- named region. Hence the snipe do not come to the Calumet, the Winnebago Swamp, the Sanga- mon, and the other favorite haunts which it frequents in Illinois, until nearly a month after they have appeared at Columbus. When they first arrive, the birds are thin and wild, and do not lie well. In a short time, however, they get very fat and become lazy. I find that in New Jersey the fall snipe-shooting is the best, and that the birds tarry so short a time in the spring that sometimes there is scarcely any spring snipe-shooting at all. Now, with us the reverse of this isthe case. The snipe stay much longer in the spring in the Western States than they do in the fall, and they distribute themselves more over the face of the country. In the autumn migration they keep more to the lines of the great rivers, and stay but a short time. One reason, no doubt, is that in the spring there is much more wet ground, such as suits the snipe. In the fall many places in which the birds lie thick in April are quite dry, and no longer suitable as feeding- places. The snipe likes wet places even more than the woodcock. His favorite resorts are wet bogs, plashy places in grassy meadows, the rich, moist ground of river-bottoms, and the margins of grassy sloughs and bayousl

" By the rushy, fringed bank,
Where grow the willow and the ozier dank!"

The best snipe-shooting with us is in the spring of the year, though very good sport may be had in the fall. In the spring I have sometimes killed from twenty-five to fifty couple a day for many days together. When the birds first come, they are poor and wild, and the shooting is difficult; but a little time spent upon the rich bottom-land, which swarms with worms and other food, puts themin flesh. They are able to indulge their sharp and almost insatiable appetite, and soon grow fat. I shot snipe several spring seasons in company with R. M. Patchen, of Atlanta, Logan County, Illinois. Our favorite ground was the Salt Creek bottoms on the Sangamon, and 1 doubt whether there is any better ground in the world. We have killed as many as three hundred and forty in a day, and our bag was seldom as small as seventy-five couple at the right time. The ground we shot over was the grassy, sedgy bottoms along Salt Creek, near where it falls into Sangamon Eiver, and across the latter stream along the bottoms in Mason County. The shooting there begins about the first of April. In many places the bottoms at that time of the year have been recently overflowed, and a scum of mud and slop is left, in which the snipe seem to delight. Snipe are vastly more abundant in the West, in the proper snipe-ground, than they are in the East. 1 find that in New Jersey and Pennsylvania snipe-shooters think they have had an average fair day's sport if they have killed about eight couple. Now, we should not think we had been shooting at all if we killed no more than that number.

A great many people go up-wind when after snipe, believing that it gives a much better chance to the dogs. I always go down-wind, and use no dog at all, except for retrieving purposes. There is no need to use a dog to find snipe on good snipe-ground at the proper times and seasons. The bird always rises against the wind, and flics up-wind or across it, making zigzags when he first gets under way. Now, if you are to windward of the bird when it rises, it is nearly certain to give you a side shot. As I remarked before, when they first come from the south in the spring, the snipe are wild. Their numbers are very large, but the ground is nearly bare, the grass having but just started. Four or five will get up together, and sometimes as many as twenty, all uttering the shrill squeak which they make on taking wing. The rich bottoms, low, marshy ground around sloughs, and wet corn-fields, are good places to look for snipe. As they eat the plump worms and other rich food which they find in abundance in the loamy soils and black, vegetable deposits, the snipe become fat, and then they lie close and well. I never found any difficulty in shooting them then. Later on in the season still they get very fat, and will hardly riseat ail, save when put up by a noise like that of their own squeak. That is the only way to make them rise, and their flight is lazy and slow. Those which remain after the first of May are then so fat that they can hardly fly at all, and when they are picked at this time they look like a lump of fat bacon. When not over-fat, snipe fly swift. They hang on the wind for an instant, and then dart away zigzag up-wind or across the wind. I have several times killed two with one barrel, and on one occasion I killed three. It was in Logan County, as I was walking along the bank of a little slough. The throe snipe got up in line, the nearest within twenty yards, and they all three fell to the right barrel. When they first come in the spring, it is difficult to shoot snipe in the corn-fields. They dodge about among the stalks, and rarely rise over the tops of them. A man who kills three out of four in the corn-fields at that time is a good shot. In shooting over the bottom-land it is best for two guns to be in company, and to walk down-wind some thirty or forty yards apart. Nearly all the birds may then be got. The shooters will be nearly certain to kill all the birds that rise between them, if they are good shots. In shooting at snipe it is a greaterror to shoot too quick. The snipe, at first getting on the wing, twists and wires in and out in his flight. If shot at then, it may be killed, but is more likely to be missed. By waiting until it has gone a rod or two you may get a much easier shot. The flight of the bird is then straight, and, though it presents but a small mark, there is no real difficulty in hitting it. Side shots are the best of all for a good shot. Beginners are somewhat apt to shoot behind the bird. The right time to pull the trigger is just as the snipe begins the direct flight. It is not a hard bird to kill on the bottoms, even while somewhat wild, if you can shoot well and go the right way about, your beat, which is downwind. Afterwards, when they have got fat, it is as easy to kill as any bird I know of. In talking with General Strong, who is a good sportsman and fine shot, and other gentlemen of Chicago, about snipe-shooting, I found" it was their impression that it was a hard bird to shoot. Now, I knew well that, taken in the right way, at the right time, it was a very easy bird to kill; and I offered to back myself to shoot and bag a hundred snipe in a hundred consecutive shots. If I missed one shot out of the one hundred, I was to be the loser. I was willing to put up the money, and to take General Strong himself as referee to see that I did it. They, however, declined to make the wager. If it had been accepted, 1 should have chosen the Salt Creek and Sangamon bottoms for the ground, and taken the last week in April for the period. The birds are then fat and lazy, and I am confident that 1 could have done the feat. I should not, as a matter of course, have bound myself to do it within a certain time, because it is not possible to say when you can find birds thick on the ground. The snipe is somewhat erratic in his habits, and change of weather causes them to change their ground. If I had found snipe on that ground as thick as I have sometimes done, I believe I should have killed the one hundred, without a miss, in one day. I should not have taken any but fair chances, and I should not have let fair shots go unimproved. In order to perform a feat of this kind a man must have several essential qualifications. He must be a dead-shot. He must have the best of nerve, and never be flurried in the least. With such a man, and a gun of ten bore, charged with five drams of powder and an ounce and a quarter of No. 12shot, the snipe rising near at hand will have but a very small chance of getting away. But as one miss will lose the wager, it is absolutely necessary that the shooter should know when he is holding his gun so that it is virtu ally certain he will kill. If I had got the match, 1 should have used no dog to shoot over, but should have walked the bottoms, going down wind, and should have chirped the snipe up with their own cry. I have often killed thirty with out a miss, when shooting for no. wager, and taking every bird that rose within fair distance, as they got up anywhere. These things may seem strange to many sportsmen, especially those who are mostly conversant with places where game is scarce and, being much disturbed and shot at, quite wild. But different localities and very different circumstances must be allowed for. I state nothing which is not true, and nothing but what I can support by good testimony|that of men who know the ground, and are acquainted with many of the anecdotes and feats 1 relate. In general snipe-shooting a man who kills two out of four is accounted a good shot, and this is generally done by beating up-wind. Now, if such a man will try my plan and beat downwind, having no dog save one to retrieve dead birds, he will find he can do much better. He will kill a great many more of the birds he shoots at. I have been snipe-shooting with men who called themselves good shots, and 1 have seen them miss full half of the birds they shot at. They almost always fired too quick, while the snipe was making his darts here and there before going off straight As a general rule, you must be willing and able to do a great deal of walking when snipe-shooting, if you would make a large bag. When I first shot snipe on Salt Creek bottoms, it was with a muzzle-loader, and I had no horse and buggy. With a horse and buggy to go to the ground and carry the bulk of the ammunition all day, and with a breech-loader, 1 could have killed three or four hundred snipe a day I could do so now if I could walk all day, as I could then; but since 1 was shot in the thigh my endurance in walking, especially on wet, slippery ground, is not as great as it formerly was. I could once walk from dawn of day till dark, only stopping to eat and drink, and could tire the best man I ever had in company in a long day's tramp after game It was upon that and upon knowledge and judgment, largely derived from experience, as to the likeliest places to find game, and how it would behave when found, that I relied in challenging any man in the world in field-shooting in the West. I counted upon these things as much as 1 did upon my ability as a marksman. My challenge stood three years, and had publicity through the sporting newspapers. There was plenty of talk about taking it up, but no one ever did so. I hear from time to time about some man who is said by some other man to be the best general field-shot in tho Western country. This best general field-shot is commonly some man who was never heard of before by me or by anybody else outside of his own small neighborhood. I believe 1 know *as* many of the real dead-shots of the West as any man in that section, and yet some one is mentioned as the best of all, of whom 1 never heard before. These foolish opinions and hollow reputations are commonly held and manufactured by those who have taken up the absurd notion that a man who is a good trap-shooter at pigeons cannot be a good field-shot. Now, the reverse of this is commonly the case. The best shots I have known at pigeons have been good shots in the field, but many men who do -well enough in the field fail at pigeons.

In snipe-shooting In the West along sloughs or wet swales, in the prairie or cornfields, there should be two guns in company, one on each side of the slough or swale. Your companion will commonly be willing that you shall take cither side you choose, as few men know that it makes any difference. But it makes a very material difference when the wind is blowing across, or nearly across, the slough, and if you take the windward side you will have the most shots. I have always done so, and have often killed two or three snipe to one killed by my companion. The reason is simply this. the snipe fly up-wind, and those which rise on the leeward side of the slough cross it to windward, while none of those which get up on the latter side fly to leeward.

When the snipe first come on in the spring, it is often primarily discovered by a certain habit they have of hovering in the air of nights, and making a kind of humming noise with their wings, as they fall from a height. I have often been out duck-shooting at night at that season of the year, and, hearing this noise in the air, have become aware that the snipe had arrived from the south. Before they leave for th"e north to breed they often do the same thing by day, and it is only when in thomood for this that snipe are on the wing by day, except when put up. When hovering, the snipe poise themselves in the air at a considerable height, and, suddenly dropping or darting away, make this noise with their wings; then they make another hover, and then another dart. When in this humor, the snipe will not lie to dogs nor to be walked up within shot, and no sport is to be had. They usually do it on still, cloudy days. I have seen statements to the effect that at such times snipe will alight on fences, stumps, and the topmost boughs of trees. I can only say, touching these statements, that my experience is all the other way. I have been many years in a part of the country where the snipe are found in amazing abundance every spring and fall; I have seen them hovering hundreds of times, when hundreds of them were at it in the air; but I never saw one alight on a tree or a fence or on anything but the ground. I have, I think, been a close observer of the habits of such game-birds as frequented Illinois. My living depended on it, in some degree. This thing, however, I never saw a snipe do, and I feel quite certain that snipe in Illinois never do it. I do not say that the authors of the statements in question have made wilful misrepresentations, but I do say that they may have been mistaken, and that the birds which alighted on trees while the snipe were hovering and bleating were not snipe. It is the easiest thing in the world to see snipe hovering in the spring in places where they abound-. Take a day in April when the sun is not bright and there is a hazy atmosphere. On such a day the snipe are at it nearly all day long. There will be first one and then another going through with this performance, and you may sometimes hear three or four at it at once, though not very close together. I have never met a man who had seen, or pretended to have seen, a snipe alight on a tree or fence at this or any other time.

Snipe begin to arrive with us in the fall, about the middle of October, but they do not come down from the north in large numbers so early as that date. At the last of October they are commonly plentiful, but are not found in the places whore they were so abundant in the spring. In the fall there are not one-fourth as many in the bottoms of Salt Creek and the Sangamon as there are in April. Neither are they so well distributed over the country along the sloughs. In going south they keep more to the lines of the bigrivers, and perhaps many of them keep more to the eastward in their southern migration than they do in coming north. I am inclined to think that this last must be the case, for the birds are not anything like as numerous in the fall, when the broods come, as they were in the spring, when the snipe went north to breed. The best fall snipe-shooting with us is along the bottoms of the Mississippi and Illinois Rivers, and about the marshes of the great Winnebago Swamp. Here the sportsman may have good shooting until late in the fallII may say, in some seasons, until the beginning of winter, for the snipe do not leave altogether until the ground is frozen. When that happens, they go southwards. In Illinois there is some marshy ground which the snipe do not like. Most of the land in that State, being rich loam or vegetable alluvial, suits them well; but in some places there is sand or gravel as well as much moisture, and neither of these does the snipe seem to like. I suppose the favorite food in these soils is scarce, and in all probability the birds do not like to bore in gritty ground. A few may be found scattered in wet places on such soils, but at the same time they lie in thousands along the loamy bottoms and in the marshes. In theselatter the soil is usually vegetable mould, the rich, black deposit commonly called swamp-muck. In this the snipe delights above all. Snipe afford a vast amount of sport, but the sport itself demands for its proper pursuit very considerable endurance and hardihood. The snipe-shooter must expect to be wet and to be fatigued, but he may also count upon making a good bag. It is one of the most delicious birds that flies, certainly second to none but the upland-plover and one or two sorts of duck. Many think it second to none whatever, and I doubt if it is when in prime order and properly cooked and served. In places where snipe are not plentiful it is no doubt advisable to use a dog to beat the meadows and marshes, and point them; but such is not the case where I have been accustomed to shoot.

8

SECTION 8

CHAPTER IX.
   GOLDEN PLOVER, CURLEW, GRAY PLOVER.
   In the West we have in the spring and fall great numbers of the golden ploverla beautiful bird, testing the skill and patience of the sportsman, and one that is very delicate and rich eating on the table. It is stated, in some books I have looked into, that the golden plover is essentially a shore bird. This is a great error, if the same species is meant, for it visits Illinois and Iowa, and I doubt not the country further west, in prodigious numbers. It is called the golden plover from being speckled with yellow on the back of the head and neck. Its principal colors are not at all like gold; and when the birds are seen in flocks on the grass-lands they love to frequent, the golden spots cannot be distinguished. It is a handsome bird, graceful in shape, and quite plump. The golden plover is not quite as large as a quail, but almost, when fat. The male is dark in color, with white spots on the breast, and narrow white streaks on the cheeks. Thefemale is gray, and a little smaller than the male. This bird winters in the south, principally upon the great grassy ranges of Texas and Northern Mexico. It arrives in the prairie States about ten days after the snipe, commonly about the tenth of April; but much depends on the forwardness or backwardness of the spring. With us there is a variation of some three weeks between a very forward spring and one that

is very late. The golden plover forms one of the most numerous bodies of the great migratory hordes which come north at the end of the winter. They come in flocks, some of the latter, on their arrival, being as many as three or four hundred in number. At their first coming they are to be found on the burnt prairies, and soon after they will be seen in ploughed fields and on bare pastures. They also frequent young wheat which is then fairly started, and in those spots where the plant has been drowned out or killed by the frost these birds are sure to be found. They like the bare earth and the close-eaten pastures, especially those in certain localities. From high knolls, where the grass has been eaten off short, they can sometimes be hardly driven away. In sheep pastures the ploverare usually found at the proper season; for the sheep is a close feeder, and likes to range on knolls and hills. Along with the golden plover, and apparently intimately associated with them and forming part of the flocks, comes the curlew, another handsome and delicious bird. It is a little larger than the golden plover, stouter in build, and gray in color. In size and shape the curlew resembles a well-grown woodcock, but with longer wings and a thinner head. It has a bill about two inches long, curved in shape, and is not so high on the leg as its companion, the golden plover. They may be easily distinguished from each other when the flock is on the ground, and also when in flight. The curlew affords as good sport to the shooter as the plover, and the epicure, who really knows how good it is, esteems it as a dish dainty and delicate as the golden plover itself, though, perhaps, not quite so delicious as the gray or upland plover, of which I shall treat further on. In the curlew there is no apparent difference between the male and female. In some flocks it will be found to be nearly as numerous as the plover, while in others the latter are in a large majority. When in the spring ploughing the rich soil of our prairie States is turned up, a vastnumber of fat worms are thrown to the surface. To pick up and feed upon these, the golden plover and curlew will be seen following the ploughman along the furrow. Sometimes they fly a little ahead of the plough and team, sometimes abreast of them, and all the time some are wheeling and curling round and dropping in the furrow which has just been made. At such times these birds occasionally become so bold and tame that they come quite close to the horses, and I have known some to be knocked down and killed by the driving-boys with their whips. As a matter of course, this is rather uncommon; but their boldness and tameness, when ploughing is going on, is in strong contrast to their timidity and wariness on other occasions. They seem to be sagacious enough to know that where the men and teams are ploughing there can be no shooting, and they take advantage of that fact.

The best places for shooting golden plover and curlew in the earlier part of their stay with us are the burnt ground of the prairies, where the grass is beginning to quicken, and those close- eaten and bare spots in the pastures of which I have made mention. It will be best, when going for these birds, to take a dog to bring in woundedones. At their first arrival the flocks of plover and curlew are rather wild and difficult to get at. In their sojourn on, and long flights from, the plains of Texas across Arkansas, and along the Mississippi River to Illinois, Missouri, Iowa, and Kansas, they have not been accustomed to the neighborhood of men, and at first they are shy. But if not shot at and frequently disturbed, they soon get tame, and may be approached. But some knowledge of their habits and some craft are always requisite in order to get good chances at these shifty and cunning birds. On some days the flocks will be much on the wing, flying from one field to another, and all going in one direction, as wild pigeons do. At such times the shooter may take a stand in the line of flight, and get fair shooting all day as the flocks go over. It is not necessary to hide altogether; in fact, in these localities|the burnt prairies and great pastures|there is seldom the means to do so; but it is often desirable to lie down. Here again it must be observed that it is of no use to lie down in clothes strongly in contrast as to color with the ground or grass. The golden plover and curlew are low-flying birds, and, when lying down in about the line of flight, the shooter maysometimes get a side shot at a large, close flock, and kill eight or ten with his two barrels. Sometimes the birds skim on not above four or five feet from the ground. At other times they fly pretty high, but within fair shot; and when one barrel of the gun is discharged, the whole flock will come swooping down towards the earth, as if the siiot had killed them all. In that case it is very difficult to put in the second barrel with good effect. When they fly low and present side shots is the most favorable time to pepper them.

At the shooting on the pastures where the birds have made their temporary home it will sometimes be found that the golden plover and curlew are not flying in flocks in one direction in such a manner that you can select a place in the line of flight. It-is then best to go with a horse and buggy. The horse should be a steady one, so as to stand fire, and should also be capable of going at a good rate, as speed is one of the elements of success in driving for plover. The birds will be seen flying about in various directions over the wide pasture, and settled in bunches on it. When put on the wing at such times, they always settle in a cluster nearly close together, and put up their head as though takinga survey of the ground. When they do this at a proper distance, the horse must be put to a swift trot in such a direction as you would take if going past the plover on your own sharp business. Judge the ground and estimate the distance, so that when you are abreast of the flock it will be within shot. The birds, in such a case, will not rise until the horse stops, and sometimes, if the shooter is quick and prompt, he may get a crack at them with one barrel juut as they are upon the point of leaving the ground, and before they are actually on the wing. When a shot can be got while they are thus huddled together, many may be killed. There is no scruple about shooting at these birds in this manner among sportsmen, but few have the art and promptness to manage it. The horse must be fast. He must trot up at a swift pace. You must judge the distance nicely, for you cannot swerve out of the line and in upon the birds without causing them to take wing. Finally, the horse must be one that will obey a light touch of the rein, and stop rather suddenly without a jerk. When shooting plover on foot at such times as they are acting after the habit described above, the sportsman must follow the same plan inprinciple. Instead of driving up, as if going by, he must run fast, as if intending to pass, and must not incline his course in towards the flock. These birds seem to act as if they reasoned and arrived at certain conclusions. These conclusions would be correct enough if the craft of the man were not exerted to deceive them by false appearances. When the shooter is abreast of the flock, he must come to a stop, and, making a quarter- whirl, fire quickly. He must be quick, for the moment he stops in his forward course up gets the flock. I never knew a man who would not thus circumvent and shoot among a flock of golden plover and curlew in this manner, if he had the skill to achieve an opportunity to do so. I have heard men say they never killed any plover except on the wing. I can readily believe it; and will add, very few in any way. All I can say is that I should not like to be the plover when these parties had a chance to put in a barrel under such circumstances as those above described. The horse and buggy is the easiest way to go to work, and that itself is somewhat difficult. The man who undertakes to run up must be swift of foot, good in the wind, and so steady of nerve that he will not be flustered and his hand will not shakewhen he stops suddenly and whirls to shoot. When, by a shot at the flock on the wing, two or three of the plover or curlew are crippled, the others will circle round them, and often offer chances for capital shots. The breech-loading gun is invaluable in such circumstances as these. On one such occasion I remember having killed forty-two golden plover and curlew, all shot on the wing, before I picked up one of them. Many a time I have killed as many as fourteen or fifteen without lifting. a bird, there being opportunities to load and fire again and again while the plover swept and circled over the dead and wounded of their own flock. Sometimes the flocks of golden plover and curlew are so numerous in a neighborhood, so large in extent, and fly in such a way, that a great number may be killed in a short time. I remember one such time well. It is now twelve years ago, and at that period there was a great deal of unbroken prairie in the neighborhood of Elkhart. I started out after dinner from thift place, and drove two miles into the prairie. It had just been burned over, and large flocks of plover and curlew were coming in one after the other. That afternoon I killed two hundred and sixty-four plover and curlew, and got back to Elkhart at sundown.I got a few sitting shots on that occasion, but the vast majority of the birds were killed on the wing, while circling round their wounded companions. This was done with a muzzle-loader. "With a good breech-loader and plenty of cartridges I believe I could have killed five hundred birds that afternoon. Much of the prairie about there, which was then unbroken, has been broken up, and is now wheat, corn, and oat land. The golden plover and curlew are not as numerous in that neighborhood now as they were then. Still, there are plenty of them in the right season of the year. Of late years I have generally killed from fifty to two hundred plover and curlew a day when out after tlicm especially. This means golden plover, as I never shoot the gray or grass plover in the spring, for a reason I shall presently advance. My bag has seldom been less than fifty, and not often as high as two hundred, and I have commonly shot right along during the season, preferring to do so rather than to go after snipe to the Sangamon and Salt Creek bottoms. The golden plover and curlew are highly esteemed by the high-livers of the cities. There is a constant demand for them at Chicago, and good prices are obtained when they first come in.

 Golden plover and curlew may be found almost anywhere in the prairie States in April. As I stated briefly in the chapters on pinnated grouse, I once went on a three months' shooting-excursion to Christian County, Illinois, starting about the first of February. My shooting companion was a hunter named Joe Phillips, and we had for camp-keeper a lively, jovial fellow named Bcti Powell. The latter has acted as camp-keeper for me many years. We pitched our tent about a couple of miles from the town of Assumption, and the report was soon spread in that primitive Western village that we were a band of gipsies. One evening a bevy of brown, blushing girls arrived at the camp and demanded information as to where the gipsy women were. They wanted to have their fortunes told, and could hardly be persuaded that we were simply hunters and of the same race of people as themselves. Afterwards some of the men of the village came, and, in conversation with Powell during the absence of Phillips and myself, boasted of a great shot they had among them. The people of the region were almost all agriculturists and herdsmen, and as for shooting game on the wing, they hardly knew what it was. The man, who had settledamong them from a distance, professed himself a great pigeon-shot. Powell listened to the wonders this man could perform, and then enquired whether they would like to back him to shoot pigeons against one of the field-shooters of our party. They said they would, and the preliminaries of a match were arranged, in which Powell was to put up our team of ponies and wagon against a hundred dollars cash on the other side. But the match was not confirmed; for while the discussion was still going on Phillips and I returned to camp from our hunt, and this broke it off'. One of the Assumption men had seen me before somewhere, and had heard my shooting well spoken of. He caused his townsmen to draw back. I have no idea that the man they spoke of was much of a shot. He very likely could not kill sixty birds in a hundred at eighteen yards rise.

During the time we shot in Christian County Phillips and 1 kept separate accounts of the game we killed. In the three months I killed with my own gun over six thousand head of game-birds. They included pinnated grouse, brant, geese, ducks, cranes, golden plover and curlew, snipe, and a few sand-snipe. The largest number were golden plover and curlew, and the next on the list was snipe.On that occasion, in one afternoon, I killed seventy-nine ducks, brant, and Canada geese; and Phillips made a good bag the same day. It sometimes falls out so that waterfowl or other birds of pursuit are so numerous and act in such a way that a very large number may be killed. These occasions do not happen, however, very often.

After the golden plover and curlew have remained with us some time in the spring, they are no longer seen in large flocks, but are found scattered and distributed over the country in small companies numbering from three or four to twelve. Early in the morning these companies are found on the bare pastures. By eight or nine in the morning they will have gone to the arable land, and are following the plough in the furrow. After they have partially dispersed in this manner they fly very fast, and then they are exceedingly good practice for the skilful shooter. The man who can make nearly certain of his single plover, flying swift, as they do, after the large flocks have broken up and scattered, is a good man at any kind of shooting. I prefer it to any other kind of practice. Before shooting against Abraham Kleinman for the championshipbadge of the United States, at one hundred pigeons each, I took two weeks' practice at plover. They were then scattered, and 1 shot at none but single birds. The practice was of much service, as the plover flew very swift and did not present a large mark. From what I could do with them in the field I was satisfied I should win the match, and it so turned out. I killed the whole of the hundred pigeons in the match; ninety-three of them were scored to me, and the other seven fell dead out of bounds. From the time the great flocks of plover scatter, which is sometimes as early as the twentieth of April, practice at single, fast-flying birds, such as I have mentioned, may be had until they go north to their breeding-grounds in the higher latitudes.

We now come to the upland or highland, grass, gray, or whistling plover, which, according to scientific naturalists, is no plover at all, strictly speaking, but a bird of similar habits and appearance, called Bartram's tatler. As it is known among sportsmen as a plover only, I shall call it one. This bird is a little larger than the golden plover, and a little longer in the leg; it is also more upright and has a longer neck than the other. Its color is gray. It is a veryhandsome bird, and neither the woods, the fields, nor the waters of the American continent supply a more delicious repast than is afforded by a dish of these rich and delicate birds. They winter upon the great plains of Mexico and Texas, upon both banks of the Rio Grande, and are in large numbers, though not so numerous as the golden plover and curlew. The upland plover is the last of the spring migrants from the south, and when it is seen with us we may safely predict that there will be no more cold weather. Its arrival in the prairie States is generally ten days later than that of the first of the united flocks of golden plover and curlew. While it lingers longer in the south than they, there is a corresponding difference in the limits of its visits to the north. They go on to higher latitudes to breed, after having stayed about a month with us. The upland plover breeds with us, though many, no doubt, go far north of Illinois to do so. Indeed, it is found in the summer in Minnesota, and Manitoba, in the British Territory. The upland plover makes a soft, whistling noise when put up, reminding one of Burns's

"Pull-toned plover gray,
Wild whistling o'er the hill."

It is a dodging, cunning bird, but, when it first arrives in the latter part of April, it is very tame and very easily shot. I never shoot it at that season, and no one ought to do so; for the birds are ready to pair as soon as they reach their breeding-grounds on our prairies. It builds in the grass of the prairie pastures, on the ground, its nest being made of dead grass, and commonly under a tussock. The eggs are a pale, bluish green, freckled with brown, and I do not think the hen usually lays more than three. I have a sort of remembrance that I have seen nests with four eggs in them, but I made no notes of them at the time, and am not quite certain. The young birds grow fast, and get fat on abundance of grasshoppers and other insects which swarm in the hot months with us. About the first of September the upland plover, young and old, are fine, plump birds, and are far more difficult to shoot than the breeding-birds were when they reached the Western States in the spring. In the fall they are wild and wary, full of craft and cunning, and hardly to be approached by a man on foot, especially if he has a gun. Almost the only way to get near enough to them to shoot is by means of a horse and buggy.They are to be found in scattered groups, we may say thin flocks, on pastures and meadows that have been mowed,. The upland plover in its flight takes much more open order than the golden plover and curlew, though still keeping a sort of companionship, and it does not settle in clusters, as is the habit of those birds. They run, scattering about over the pastures and meadows, catching grasshoppers and such like insects, and, when put up, they fly ofl' swift, in open order, well spread out. The sportsman who is after them with the horse and buggy must pursue the same tactics as those mentioned in reference to shooting golden plover and curlew in the spring. The horse must go fast, and the man must shoot the moment he stops. I never try to step to the ground, but shoot from the buggy. It is best to have a companion when after these wild and wary birds. While one men lies down in a selected spot, the other drives round to the far side of the birds, and gets his shot if he can. Whether he does or not, the plover will be apt to fly over the man lying down. This is the only system which promises any success for men who are after upland plover on foot in the fall of the year. It is of no use chasing after themover the meadows and pastures, in hopes to get near enough for a shot.

Sand-snipe and grass snipe (so-called in the West) are not snipe, but some sorts of tatlers or sand-pipers. They resemble the plover, but are smaller, being only about the size of a true snipe. The sand-snipe has a whitish breast; the grass-snipe is a gray bird. They come about the same time as golden plover and curlew, and in pretty large flocks. In dry seasons these flocks appear to unite, two or three making but one, and then they are in very large numbers together. They are nice, plump birds, as good to eat as plover, and easy to get at. However, good as they are, few people shoot them,- and it is easy enough to get within range of a flock of them. They frequent marshy ground, such as the true snipe likes. Unlike the latter, however, they fly in flocks, and settle down, clustered together, on the muddy edges of sloughs and little water-holes, which they see while crossing the prairie on the wing. Once, when I was out shooting golden plover and curlew, 1 saw a great flock of these smaller birds in a marshy spot near a little pond. 1 thought they were plover, but as I neared them the flock rose, and then I saw it was a vast col-

lection of sand-snipe. It was a dry season, and, as is then their wont, they had gathered into great flocks. They flew around, and finally settled again. 1 do not usually trouble myself with this bird, for nobody seems to care about it, although it ia as good eating as the snipe itself, for all the long bill of the latter; but as I had come down to them, 1 concluded to take a crack at the flock. It was certainly as much as five hundred in number. So I let fly with one barrel charged with No. 10, and, making a raking shot over the ground, killed fifty-four. If game were scarce with us, as it is in some parts, sand-snipe and grass-snipe would be held in esteem,

9

SECTION 9

CHAPTER X.
WILD DUCKS AND WESTERN DUCK-SHOOTING.

The best of the ducks which are found in the Western States are Canvas-backs, Redheads, Mallards, Pintails, Blue-bells, Blue and Green winged Teal, Widgeon, and Black Ducks. There are also Wood-ducks, which, though most beautiful in plumage, are not very fine on the table. Some are, however, shot for the sake of their feathers, which are exported to England, where the brilliant hues of part of their plumage are used in the manufacture of artificial flies for salmon and trout fishing. And besides the species mentioned above, there are two or three ducks of other sorts, which, being scarce and comparatively worthless, are of no account to the sportsman, and need not be further alluded to in this work. The wood-duck breeds in Illinois and the other Western States along the rivers and creeks, and always in or on the edge of timber. It is rather numerous along the Sangamon and the shores of Salt Creek. They make their nests in hollows of trees, and are theonly kind of ducks which, to my knowledge, ever alight in trees. It is very beautiful, having gorgeous plumage, with a topknot on the head. The female hatches from eight to twelve young in a brood, and carries them off one by one to the water. The wood-duck is short, small, and stout, weighing about a

Field, Cover, and Trap Shooting. Adam H. Bogardus

pound and a half, and is not much prized for the table. It is very swift in flight, and can go through timber like a wild pigeon or a ruffed grouse.

Of the ducks to be found with us, the most numerous, and perhaps the best, is the mallard. I consider it quite equal to the canvas-back in juiciness and flavor, and also to the redhead or pochard. Jt is true that so much has been written and said about the unrivalled excellence of the canvas-back that it may seem heretical to maintain that the mallard is as good. Such, however, is my own conviction; and though some say that the canvas-backs of the West have not the peculiar flavor of those procured on the sea-coast iu shallow waters, others, whose experience of them in both localities is large, say this is an error, arising from prejudice and imagination. The editor of this work states some facts which go to fortify me in my opinion. He says that whenSenator Pugh was in Washington, representing the State of Ohio, this question of the superiority of the canvas-backs of the East over those which had fed and got fat on the wild rice and wild celery of the West was mooted at a supper in which canvas-backs were the chief dish. All those practically unacquainted with the Western ducks laughed at the notion that they could compare in excellence with those of Maryland. Mr. Pugh was rather deaf, as he always has been, but he seems to have hoard the observations in question, though he did not contradict them then. He wrote, however, to a friend of his, then collector at San- dusky, on the shallow bay of that name in Lake Erie, a noted resort for Western wild fowl, requesting him to send to Washington a few couple of fat canvas-backs. In due time they arrived, and the gentlemen of the party who had met before were invited by the senator to supper. He had procured some fine canvas-backs from Baltimore, and ho took good care his guests should know it. But before the ducks were cooked those from Ohio were substituted for those of the Patapsco. They were served up, eaten with great relish, and the usual pseans of praise, and not a man at the table except Senator Pughknew that they had feasted on Western ducks until told so the next day. Even then they were hardly convinced. Another matter in this connection is that the very able and well-informed author, Dr. Sharpless, of Philadelphia, stated that he could never distinguish much difference in flavor between canvas-backs and redheads, and that many of the latter were sold as canvas-backs and eaten as such by those who professed to know all about the divine flavor. The editor of this work has often received canvas-back ducks from Mr. Saliagnac, of Philadelphia, who rents shootings on the coast. The canvas-backs sent to him by that gentleman were in truth very excellent, but neither he nor any one else who partook of them thought them superior to some mallards which had been killed in a wheat-stubble in Iowa, and were sent on as a present by Mr. James Bruce, of Keokuk, now of St. Louis, Missouri. Moreover, Mr. Saliagnac himself, great sportsman and enthusiastic admirer of canvas-backs as he is, told the editor that his breed of tame ducks, the large, white upland Muscovy, were just about as fine eating as canvas-backs when fattened and killed at the right time, and cooked in the same way. Of course all this will be hooted at by thosewho have made the wonderful, exquisite, unparalleled excellence of the canvas-back a matter of superstition. It is indeed as excellent as any duck, and for luscious richness the ducks at least equal any other description of bird. The canvas- back is a great deal better in proportion to the praises heaped upon it than the brook-trout is; for whatever sport they may give to the angler, the " speckled beauties" arc nothing like as good to eat as many other fish not thought much of. Fashion, however, goes a great way in these matters, and few are as candid as the Irishman, who, having gone some distance in a sedan-chair without a seat, replied, in answer to the question how he liked it:

" Faith, but for the name of the thing I might as well have walked !"

The mallards winter in the south for the most part, though a few remain on the Sangamon all the cold season, unless the weather is very intense and the frost so long continued and rigid as to freeze up all the springy pools of that river. When they come north in the spring, a few remain with us and make their nests in the Winnebago Swamp and the bottoms of the Sangamon Eiver and Salt Creek. But the vast majority, after remaining with us some time, go still further north to breed and rear their young. Their northern limit is in a very high latitude. The mallard is the most beautiful of all ducks, except the wood-duck, and naturalists are agreed that the common breeds of domesticated ducks have sprung from the former. It crosses readily enough with tame ducks, to my knowledge, and the produce of the cross are prolific, though wild and apt to go away with the wild mallards ia the fall. The mallards with us make their nests about the middle of April in an average season. When out snipe-shooting about the 1st of May, I have found mallards' nests already containing seven or eight eggs. The nests are built near the water in some secluded marsh or lonely swamp, on tussocks of grass near the edges of sloughs, and in wet river-bottoms. And sometimes I have found the nest of the mallard on the margin of a pond in the prairie or the pasture fields. The nest is nicely made of dry grass and sedge, and by the time the female is ready to sit it is lined with soft, loose feathers, just as the nest of the tame duck is. The eggs are from twelve to sixteen in number, in color of a greenish blue cast, and very much like thoseof the tame ducks which lay greenish blue eggs. The eggs of some sorts of tame ducks are a shining white, as if glazed. The broods of young mallards, the flappers, are first seen about the 10th of June. There are commonly from eight to twelve in a brood. The little things are active and cunning from the first. If they are pursued, they dart swiftly under water, and, swimming beneath to the bank, just put their bills above the surface and lie quiet. When they are somewhat bigger, they go out upon the margins of the streams and ponds, and hide in the grass. About the middle of October the young mallards are full grown and well feathered so as to be able to fly fast and far. The drake is a little larger than the duck, and a large one will weigh nearly three pounds. Widgeon and the two kinds of teal also breed with us to some extent, but their nests are seldom found. In the Winnebago Swamp there are a few nests of the broadbill or spoonbill. The pintail does not breed with us, and 1 believe not on this side of the arctic regions.

If the winter is broken, the ducks begin to arrive from the south by the middle of February, and in an early spring they are found inthousands by the 1st of March. When they first come to the prairie States in the spring, they are in poor condition, but after feeding about tho corn-fields a short time they become plump and fat. Ducks, wild and tame alike, are great feeders, and will be found eating in the evening long after other birds have gone to roost. The mallards and pintails fly from their roosting-places on the water to the fields at early morning, and on wet, cloudy days remain in the corn-fields all day. They are so numerous that the fields appear at such times to have ducks scattered all over them. On clear days they do not remain in the fields on the feed all day, but return to their haunts on the water about nine or ten o'clock. In the afternoon they fly to the corn-fields again about three or four o'clock, when they first come from the south; but after being with us some time their evening flight to the fields is not made till sundown, and sometimes not till it is nearly dark. The mallards are then paired off, but not so the pintails. When not in the corn-fields, both kinds are about rivers and ponds.

The blue-winged teal and the green-winged, with the widgeon, use more about sloughs andstreams. They do not come into the corn-fields much, and are shot along rivers and creeks. I have, however, seen these small ducks flying to the corn-fields when it was nearly dark. At times, when ponds in corn-fields are enlarged by rains, and the low places in the fields are overflowed, many teal resort to them. From such places, at break of day, I have often put up hundreds of teal and hundreds of other kinds of ducks. A great many teal and small ducks, such as blue- bills, are shot on the Calumet River, and Abe Kleinman gets his full share of them. Mallards, canvas-backs, and red-heads are sometimes shot there too, but the smaller ducks are those which commonly prevail. The spring ducks remain with us from four to five weeks, but after the great multitudes have gone north some straggling parties still remain. Mallards pair by the middle of March, and the teal next. The other kinds of ducks are later, and 1 do not think they have paired up to the time of their leaving our latitudes for the higher ones in which they breed in most cases.

About the last of September the ducks begin to arrive from their breeding-grounds in the far north. Some are seen before that time, but theyare those which have stopped with us to breed, and the broods they have produced. There is no great abundance from the arrivals until pretty sharp frosts have set in, which is generally about the middle of October, but some seasons not till later. Still the main body seems to hold off, and it is not until cold weather has set in fairly that the ducks come in vast numbers. Then they may be heard all night flying to the southward in large flocks, and a great many alight and tarry by the way. Sometimes the whole country appears to swarm with them. In places on tho prairies and the great pastures where corn in the ear is dumped down by wagon- loads to feed bullocks, I have seen acres thickly covered with Canada geese, brant geese, mallards, and pintails. As a rule, shooting is not allowed in such places, because it scares the cattle; but the owners and herdsmen have sometimes shifted their droves to another place, in order to give me a chance to shoot the wild fowl congregated thereabouts. Then I have had grand spots.

The fall ducks remain until the country is mostly frozen up; and in an open fall they are with us in large numbers until nearly Christmas.Some mallards stay on the Sangamon all the winter, unless the season happens to be particu-. larly severe and the cold very steady and intense. When the fall ducks arrive, they are in fine condition, having fed on the wild rice of the north, and the young mallards are delicious eating at that time. I know of nothing better, and -of hardly anything else as good.

Duck-shooting is often rough, wet work. About the rivers and sloughs it is necessary to be more or less in the water, unless the shooter has a boat; besides which, the ducks secured are necessarily wet and draggled. Shooting ducks in the corn-fields, as they come to feed, is different. The shooter can usually manage to keep tolerably dry, and the ducks shot fall on the ground instead of in the water. But even then it requires considerable fortitude and much skill and patience. People who want to sit by the fire on cold, wet days, when the wind blows strong and keen, are not cut out for duck- shooters. When I go out for duck-shooting on their feeding-grounds, I first ascertain by observation the fields they are flying to and from, and the places they cross the bounds at. Ducks are like sheep in some respects. Where one flock flies the others follow, keeping the same general route, unless they see something to make them swerve from it. I then select the best spot I can find to lie down in that is, the one most screened from observation and beneath the line of flight. A rubber blanket being spread, down I go on my back, in clothes the color of the grass or ground I lie on. This is an essential point. It is useless to expect the ducks to continue their flight over an object in dark clothes lying upon faded grass, or over a man in light clothes lying upon black ground. My shooting suit is corduroy, with a cap of the same; and as it is about the color of the grass, cornstalks, and weeds late in the fall, it answers very well. If the shooter has no corduroy clothes, let him wear a linen duster over his dark clothes. The latter may do very well for a patch of black ground in a corn-field, or a dark ground at a crossing-place; but usually corduroy can be made to suit anywhere by a little care in selection, because dead grass and weeds nearly everywhere prevail. A man in dark clothes by a pond in the prairie would not get a duck in a day, no matter how numerous they might be in the neighborhood. Ducks are wary birds and very far-sighted. But some men seem to believe that the ducks are as foolish and as thoughtless as themselves. They post themselves in places where the color of their clothes is in strong contrast with everything else around; and when the ducks sheer off wide as soon as they see them, the shooters in question blaze away out of distance, and never touch a feather. I have been out with men under circumstances in which they said that the ducks all came to me as if they knew me. The simple cause of it was that I lay down in a suit of corduroy, and they were stretched out in clothes black enough for a funeral. If a man going to shoot ducks on the prairie, by the ponds and sloughs, has no corduroy clothes and no duster, let him go to the grocery- store and get a coffee-sack or two to make a smock. That material is just the right color.

In regard to corn-fields,- it must be noted that the ducks appear to frequent those most in which the stalks are broken down. In these no blind can be made. If one is made, the ducks will not come near it. The shooter must be down on his back, his feet towards the quarter from which the ducks are coming, and wait until they get over him. In a field where the corn-stalks are still standing a thin blind may be made of them, but more ducks, other things being equal, will be killed in the broken-down corn without a blind than in the other with one. When the shooter sees the ducks coming, he must not move himself, nor must he move his gun, which young beginners always have a strong inclination to do. If the man moves, the ducks approaching in the air see his movement. If the gun is moved, they catch the glance of the light upon it in time to sheer off and balk the idle discharge of the too impatient shooter. When the ducks are seen coming, the man on the ground should lie quite still until they are over him, or almost over him. He should then rise quickly to a sitting posture, at which they will check their forward flight, and tower up into the air. That is the right time to shoot I may say the only time, in this description of the sport, in which there is a real good chance of killing. He who is trying for ducks in this way must not expect to be able to get on his feet to shoot. If he tries to do so, he will kill no ducks. He who cannot rise to a sitting posture from his back and shoot that way must wait for the ducks on his hands and knees, and shoot kneeling. It does not much matter which of these modes is adopted|although lying on the

10

SECTION 10

back is the best of the two|but it is essential that the shooter should make no move until the ducks are nearly over him. It is also absolutely necessary that his clothes should be of the color of the ground he lies on, for otherwise the ducks never will be over him. I have killed many thousands, and consider these to be the great points upon which the sport depends. When there is snow on the ground, the overdress of the shooter should be white, or nearly white, and a white handkerchief should be tied over his cap. At times when there is snow on the ground the ducks resort largely to the corn-fields, and the sport in them at such times is usually very good, provided the shooters carry it on in the right way.

CHAPTER XI.
DUCKS AND WESTERN DUCK-SHOOTING.

In the spring of the year, after the ducks have come from their wintering-places, there is often some very cold weather, and, though all but the running streams are frozen over, the wild fowl never go back again, if they can possibly avoid it. Their instinct is very strong against turning to the southward at that season of the year. At such times, and at any other times, when the ice is thick, a good blind may be built of it near the open water, and much sport may be had. The shooter must of course expect to be cold, and he will be very cold while waiting for ducks in hard weather, especially when he waits a long time in vain. But the coming in of the ducks in good flights raises the spirits, stimulates the circulation of the blood, and revives the warmth of the body. I have sometimes got so cold that I could hardly charge my muzzle-loading gun; but good sport soon changed that. The shooting along the Illinois River is very good indeed, and there are more canvas-backs and red-heads there than there are about the Sangamon or in the neighborhood of Elkhart; but my favorite among ducks, whether for sport or the table, is the plump, heavy, beautiful mallard.

As I remarked before in alluding to the color of the duck-shooter's clothes, ducks know a good deal more than some of the men who go after them. You may see some of the latter select for their shooting-place a corn-field in which the stalks are all broken down, and there they go to work and build a standing blind of the stalks. " In vain is the net of the fowler spread in sight of the bird." The ducks have probably flown over that field dozens of times, and noticing this blind|a thing there new and strange| they sheer off from it instead of flying on to go over it or near it, and the man inside of it gets no shots within killing distance. When I see that a man has built a blind in such a place, I just take advantage of his ignorance and folly by going and lying down some hundred and fifty or two hundred yards on one side of it. All the ducks that sheer off from it on that side I get a shot at. In this way I have often

killed twenty or thirty, while the man in the blind never got a duck. Sometimes the man in the blind seeing this would make shots out of all distance, more for the purpose of scaring the ducks from me than with any hope of bringing them down himself. When that has been the case, I have left him to his own devices, and gone to another part of the field altogether. It is necessary to remark for the information of Eastern readers that the corn-fields of Illinois are commonly very large, and not like the small enclosures of the Atlantic States. The former sometimes contain as much as a thousand afres without any intervening fence. Production on this great scale tends to keep game plentiful in two or three ways. The farm-houses are far apart, which is one thing. As long as the corn-stalks are standing green these fields afford capital cover for pinnated grouse and quail, as remarked heretofore. Another thing is that they afford abundance of food for grouse, quail, turkeys, geese, ducks, etc. Some parts of the summer the birds get a plentiful supply of insects in the corn. In the fall of the year and winter, and in the following spring, the grouse, geese, and ducks feed largely on the corn itself, there being always some scattered about, even in the fields from which the ears have been hauled off.

Duck-shooting in the corn-fields in the fall is fine, pleasant sport. At that season many of the stalks are still standing, and plenty of places may be found to hide. Besides, the ducks are not then very wild, and the majority of them are young birds which, not having been shot at a great deal, are not as wary as the old stagers, who remember the shooting on their passage north in the spring. An excellent place at this time of the year is on the windward side of an Osage orange hedge, near where they cross on their way to feed. When the wind is blowing against them, ducks fly low. With the wind nearly dead ahead of them, the shooter on the windward side of the hedge will get plenty of shots at low-flying ducks as they come over, and need not take the trouble to lie down in the corn at those times. Rainy, misty, windy weather is the best of weather for this method. On such days the ducks are flying low and going into and out of the corn-fields all day. In clear weather they fly higher, but still low in their evening flights, coming out to feed. Sometimes the flocks will be seen high in the air, as itsetting *out* on a long migratory flight; but coming over a corn-field, they will sail around, shut their wings, and come sloping to the ground. Ducks generally sweep round in a circle before settling down. A pond or little slough in a corn-field is a capital place to lie for ducks. The shooter must Jie down on the bank, as in other places. 1 have killed from three to four dozen ducks in an evening's shooting in a cornfield, and that often.

One thing I have noticed which will be of great importance to beginners in duck-shooting. It is that they always seem to be nearer than they really are when in flight. Allowance must be made by the shooter for this deceptiveness of appearance as to distance. When 1 have killed a duck, I have often been surprised to find how far it fell from me. One that seemed to be but thirty yards off' would turn out to be forty-five. It was not the momentum of flight after being hit that could account for this, as such ducks had commonly stopped in their forward progress, and were towering up when shot at. Ducks also seem to be lower than they really are when seen in flight, and this is especially the case in some sorts of weather. In some states of the atmosphere they will seem to bemuch nearer than at other times when the distance is actually the same. In nine cases out of ten, when a man shoots at ducks flying over him, they are higher in the air than he believes them to be. 1 have often seen men fire at ducks which were so high and so far off that the flock would not change its direction at the report, and just kept on, seemingly looking down contemptuously on the foolish shooter. In the spring of the year and late in fall, when the ducks are heavily feathered, a side shot is best for penetration, as it may take effect under the wing. When shooting from a blind, it is best to let the ducks pass a little before firing. When the shooter is lying on the ground, the turn made by the ducks as they tower up gives better chance of penetration; but the grand secret of penetration is a hard-hitting gun of good weight and calibre, and plenty of powder.

In the prairies there are many ponds and sloughs, and the waters are generally well up in them when the prime of the time for shooting ducks comes in the spring and fall. At such places it is advisable to use decoys, and with these well set out a man may shoot on and off all day when the ducks are flying about. Wooden
jdecoys, painted to represent ducks, are used by many people, but I prefer something different, more natural than the joiner and painter can turn out. I have killed hundreds of dozens of ducks shooting over decoys, and the best I ever used were tame ducks of the color of the mallard. Three of these, a drake and two ducks, I used to fit with a piece of leather on the leg, and a string five or six yards long for each. I then staked them out in shallow water, so that they could not come nearer than four or five feet of the bank, and lay down. They were, in my opinion, much better than any dead decoy, whether duck or wood. After being used as decoys for some time these ducks seemed to understand what was required of them, and to enter into the business with interest. They would swim about and play, and 1 had one pair that would call to the wild mallards when they saw them goin over.

The next best thing to these tame live decoys for the waters of which I am writing is the dead mallard itself. As soon as I got a couple, when not employing the tame

ducks, I put them out, and sometimes I have had as many as fifteen dead ducks out as decoys together. Sue-
cess greatly depends upon the way in which they are set out; though set out in the most artful and natural manner, they are not as effectual as tame ducks of the mallard color, because these last swim about, and the ducks flying above see them in motion. I have sometimes killed as many as seventy or eighty ducks in a day's shooting with decoys of dead ducks. My method of setting them out was as follows: Having killed the duck and got him on the bank, take a stick, or, on the prairie where there are no sticks, a reed, or the stalk of a strong weed, which is there big and stiff. Sharpen one end to a point, which insert under the skin of the duck's breast and along up the neck, just beneath the skin, into the head. Do this so that the head holds a natural position to the body, and the neck is not awry. Then wade out and plant the other end of the stick in the mud over which there is a foot of water or a little more. The body of the duck must then rest on the water, as that of a live duck does, and, after having smoothed the feathers nicely, the shooter returns to his lying-down place on the bank. It is best to keep on setting these dead decoys until you have seven or eight out; and if you largely in-
srease the number, it will be simply all the better. I make no blind by the pond or slough, but lie on the grass, unless there is brush or a growth of willow to hide in. Neither do I ever wait for the ducks to settle, but shoot while they are still on the wing. One day at Skunk's Island, in the great Winnebago Swamp, I killed a hundred and thirty ducks over dead-duck decoys set out after the plan I have described, and in that day's shooting I never hid at all. I sat on a muskrat-house all the time, sometimes, however, lying down. It made no difference whether I lay or sat, for the ducks were flying thick, and in the humor to " come and be killed," as the old song has it, which says:

" Old Mother Bond got up in a rage,
Her pockets full of onions, her lap full of sage ;
And she went to the pond, did old Mother Bond,
Crying, ' Dill, dill, dill! dill, dill, dill!

Come and be killed !
The guests are all met, their bellies must be filled.'"

On the occasion to which I have alluded I was out of ammunition before night. It was late in the fall, when large flocks fly, and two or three ducks may sometimes be killed by one barrel.The place called the Inlet, at the east end of the swamp, some miles from Skunk's Island, is famous ground for ducks. The Winnebago Swamp is very extensive. What h called the Outlet runs into Green River, all along which stream there is very good duck-shooting. In the big pastures, which are sometimes four or five miles long and one or two miles wide, there are often ponds at which the bullocks being fatted for market drink. At these ponds great shooting over decoys is often to be had. On Mr. Sullivant's great farm in Ford County there are many ponds and many extensive corn-fields, and I found last spring that the shooting of geese, ducks, and crane there was very good lso good that I mentally resolved to go there again next season. In two days' shooting, mornings and evenings, not over decoys, but as the wild fowl came to and went out of the corn-fields, I killed sixty-five mallards and pintails, mostly mallards, five brant geese, twenty sand-hill crane, and three large white crane. Yet I was told that the ducks and brant had mostly all gone north before I was there, and that they had been much more abundant than they were in the two days I shot. Mr. Sullivant's foreman saw my ducks and cranes at the station, and made his remarks to this effect: " They said that as you were a pigeon-shooter, you would not be successful in the field. I have, however, seen no such lot as that at any time this season, and yet the ducks are now scarce to what they have been."

This farm of Mr. Michael Sullivant's is the largest in Illinois, I think, and I am convinced that it is one of the best neighborhoods in the State for game. From what I saw, pinnated grouse abound, there are lots of quail, and in the migratory seasons great flocks cf ducks, geese, brant, and cranes. The estate was purchased by Mr. Sullivant some years ago, when it was mostly unbroken prairie. It is eight miles square, contains about forty-four thousand acres, and twenty-six thousand acres of it have already been brought under cultivation. Twenty thousand acres of it were in corn last year, and I dare say more will be this year, while three thousand acres were in smaller grain, and three thousand in meadow-grass. Mr. Sullivant, the owner and farmer of this extensive and fertile tract, was formerly the largest landowner in Franklin County, Ohio, and very likely is so still. His father was one of the first settlers near Columbus, the capital of Ohio; in fact, he lived just west of the Scioto River, opposite where the State House now stands, before there was a house in Columbus at all; and his younger sons, Joseph and William, still reside in that city. The Illinois proprietor is the eldest son of the old pioneer. The family is famous for culture, enterprise, and the uncommon personal beauty of its members. They are a tall, powerful, handsome race ; and probably in all the vast regions of the West not a tribe excels this family, in all its branches, in stature, symmetry, strength, and beauty. Upon this Illinois farm there are three hundred miles of Osage orange hedges, which are yet young. Let the sportsmen remember what has been said of the hedges as affording nesting- places for game-birds, protection against hawks, and facilities for shooters, and they may conceive what these three hundred miles of hedges will do when they have grown tall and thick. Now to come back to the ducks.

On the large streams, such as the Mississippi and Illinois rivers, it is commonly necessary for the duck-shooter to use a boat, and it is hardly practicable to use any but decoys of wood, painted to represent the sort of ducks expected. Upon these rivers I have killed canvas-backs, red-heads, mallards, and some few black or dusky ducks.I have not been out much on these large rivers, however, but have shot more in the corn-fields, on the sloughs and ponds about the prairies, in and about the Great Winnebago Swamp, and on the Sangamon and Salt Creek. Sometimes when a man is out after other sorts of shooting, especially snipe, he will find that the ducks are in such numbers, and flying in such a way, that he may abandon his intended pursuit, and turn his attention to them. His shot will be smaller on such occasions than he would have chosen for ducks; but with plenty of powder to drive them at high velocities, he will get penetration, and bring the wild fowl down. Once upon Salt Creek, near where it falls into the Sangamon, I was out after snipe, and noticed that the mallards were flying in such a way as to afford a fine chance. 1 had nothing but No. 9 shot, but determined to try what could be done. This was in 1868. The edge of the creek was well timbered, and, choosing my post, I seated myself on a log among the trees and brush. There was a light snow on the bottoms some three inches deep, and the snipe had to get near the margins of the streams to feed. I could have killed a good bag of them, but the ducks offered a chancemuch too tempting to be neglected. I could not forego the opportunity, and sitting upon that log, and shooting as they flew until all my ammunition was expended, I killed and secured ninety- five mallards. Some few, which fell on the other side of the creek, I did not get. With plenty of cartridges and a breech-loader I believe 1 could have killed two hundred ducks. They were all mallards. The date was April 7. Most of the mallards flew in pairs, and their route was towards the north. 1 have no doubt they were beginning their migratory flight from our neighborhood to the high latitudes.

In hard, severe weather, when the wind is strong and keen-cutting, it is to be noted that ducks and other water-fowl are apt to seek the protection of the timber. At such times they will be found in creeks whose banks are well wooded, and about ponds hi the timber. In these places the shooter need not go to the trouble of building a blind. There are in such situations so many old logs, stumps, etc., that if he sits down in clothes of the proper color, the ducks will not make him out in time to change the direction of their course in flight. Thus on the great day at Skunk's Island, in the WinnebagoSwamp, and on that of Salt Creek, I had no blind, and did not hide myself in any particular manner. In the first case I sat on a muskrat house all the time; in the second I was seated on an old log while all the shooting was done. It is, however, necessary that the shooter should keep still; for the ducks will see any movement a long way off, and they know that stumps of trees and the like do not move. In cold weather, when the ducks seek the timber for shelter, they fly very fast; he who can kill three out of every four shots he makes is a good marksman, and will have all the ducks he will want to carry far on his back.

11

SECTION 11

CHAPTER XII
   WILD GEESE, CRANES, ANS SWAN,
   Among the wild geese to be $/ .d in the spring and fall in the States of tho great Mississippi Valley, there are at least two varieties which are common in the same seasons Gj the seaboard of the Atlantic States. These ie the Canada goose, the common wild goose, known almost everywhere, and the brant goows. But besides these, we have in the Western States vast numbers of small geese of other varietu.o, which we commonly call Mexican geese. As raany as three of these differ in their plumage, wid, though found in the same flocks apparently, are no doubt the following : Ilutchinson's Goose, the V.Thite-Fronted Goose, and the Snow Goose. As t.entioned above, they are only known by Western sportsmen as Mexican geese. We have, then, five or six varieties of wild geese in Illinois, Lwa, etc. Of these tho, Canada goose is the largest and finest, and it used to be much the rrost numerous. It is a handsome bird, weighing when fat from ten to fourteen pounds. It winters in the south, and on its passage towards the north does not stay with us a great while, though a few remain all the summer, and I have seen the nest of this goose in the Winnebago Swamp. Their great breeding- grounds are far to the north of any of the habitations of white men, or even of Indians. They have been seen above the latitude of eighty north, and were

even then flying on towards the pole. In those solitary regions, during the brief arctic summer, the several kinds of wild geese rear their young in vast numbers, and, when in the fall they set out upon their southerly migration, they fly in innumerable flocks. They usually fly high, and, though their flight seems to be labored, it is very swift for so heavy a bird. In foggy weather their flight is low, and they appear to be confused, as if uncertain of the proper route. They intermix freely with tame geese, and the cross is much esteemed for its size and excellence on the table. Canada geese are rather easily domesticated, but even then the instinct of migration northward in spring is so strong that they get uneasy. Sometimes when not pinioned they rise into the air and join flocks going over, and sometimes they wander off and are shot as wild geese. A cross of the Canada goose no doubt improves the domestic goose in beauty and flavor, if not in size, and it is easy to procure it by means of wounded ganders, pinioned and turned down with the tame geese.

The Canada goose is not so abundant in Illinois in the migratory seasons as it used to be. When I first settled in that State, there were vast flocks of these geese all over the country in the spring and late in the fall. In the daytime they were mostly in the sloughs and bottoms, and there they roosted at night, but they came out mornings and evenings to feed. They are very fond of corn, and consume large quantities of it. The reason why they are now less abundant in Illinois is the thicker settlement of the country. The main column of the Canada geese now take a more westerly route towards the south, crossing Minnesota, Kansas, Nebraska, Iowa, and the country up the Missouri River. But there are a great many in Illinois still at the right times of the year. The Canada goose comes earliest of all the great tribes which migrate from the south in the spring, and, considering that most of them have to fly over a space covering more than fifty degrees of latitude before they reach their breeding-places, it may be supposed they cannot stop very long with us in their vernal flights. As to the few which remain all the winter on the Sangamon River and in other wild places where there may be open water, they are too insignificant to count for much. The Canada geese come in their great flocks in February, with the first freshet or open weather, and remain till the middle of March, as a rule, while a few linger along until April comes. They come before any of the ducks, and they go on north before them. The Winnebago Swamp is a great resort for the wild geese. Formerly. they used to breed there in considerable numbers, but of late years their nests in that quarter have been few. They may, however, still be found by those who penetrate into the marshy recess they choose for their breeding-places.

When the wild geese arrive in the spring, they are commonly lean, but, after having fed on corn for a little space, they gain flesh and become in good order. A favorite .resort of theirs in the spring is the great pasture-lands. Upon these thousands of bullocks have been fed all winter on corn in the ear. Bullocks are wasteful feeders, and much corn lies shelled around. This the geese pick up and fatten upon. In such places the flocks alight in the middle of the wide pastures, and are very hard to get at. Oftentimes the first notice we have of the arrival of the wild geese is their hoarse call in the air, as they fly by night. When great flocks of the various kinds of wild geese are coming north in spring, or going south at the near approach of winter, they may be heard calling to and answering each other nearly all night long. The Sangamon used to be a capital place for wild geese, and there is still good shooting there.

The best situation for the shooter is behind a hedge or in a bunch of weeds at a fence near their crossing-places as they go to feed. It is best when they are flying to windward. The wild geese have regular crossing-places, and these may be easily ascertained by watching the flights of the flocks. The shooter must go to his station very early in the morning, before they begin to fly. They fly very early, especially if the weather is warm and pleasant. In cold, windy weather they are later. Commonly they are on the wing about break of day, and I have seen them flying when it was still so near dark that I could hardly tell whether a flock was Canada geese, brant geese, or the so- called Mexican geese. When the wild geese comeover their crossing-places well in the air, the shooter must find some means of concealment. If there is no hedge under which to crouch down, he must lie on the dead grass or in the weeds, with clothes of the proper color to deceive the geese and elude the watchful eyes of their leaders. The weeds are often three feet high and thick, and in these cover for the shooter may be found. He must keep quite still until the geese, windward bound, are right over him. If he does not do so, his movement will be seen, he will hear the cry which gave notice to the sleeping Romans of the stealthy footsteps of the Gauls, and he will find, whether he shoots or not, that the geese have saved the Capital. On windy mornings wild geese fly very low, often not more than fifteen or twenty feet from the ground. In calm, clear weather they are much higher. Nothing can be done at the hedges and fences in such weather, and the shooter must then go to the corn-fields where they feed.

A field in which the corn is cut up and shocked affords a promising chance. The shooter may build a little house of corn-stalks like a shock, in the row of shocks, and get inside of it. Some men get behind a corn-shock, but the plan is not a good one. Ill circling round the field one of thegeese sees him, and the others keep away, sheer off wide. The little blind made like a shock of corn is best, but it must be made ready in the daytime, or in the night season before the geese have begun to fly. In wet, misty weather the wild geese remain about the corn-fields all day, and then from a blind properly made the very best shooting may be had. I have killed eleven Canada geese before breakfast in one of Mr. Gillott's corn-fields, not more than a mile and a half from Elkhart. I went out to the field on horseback, and tethered my horse to a fence.

In windy weather the best shooting is at the crossing-places, and the shooter must choose his place and method according to the weather. On the large pastures the best plan is to use a horse and buggy. The wild geese may be seen sitting in the pastures and in the prairie when they are a long way off. The shooter must drive briskly on, as if he was going past them, on the windward side, gradually drawing nearer, but never heading directly towards them. If he does the latter, the flock will fly, although he may be as much as two hundred yards from them. When the shooter is opposite the geese, he pulls up the horse with one hand, drops the reins, and raiseshis gun. The geese start to fly, but they cannot rise down-wind, and, getting up against it, as they must do, they come towards the gun. Then is the time to fire; but beware of miscalculating the distance. Geese look very large on the prairie. I have seen men shoot at geese, believing them to be within killing distance, when they were certainly not less than two hundred yards away. I have also seen them fired at in flight when they were so high in the air that they passed without noticing the shot. Yet a goose may be killed at a great distance with large shot if it happens to be hit in a vital part.

I once killed one at a hundred and nineteen yards with a BB cartridge. The ground was measured, as I knew it was a very long shot. It was a chance shot. I had driven on the flock two or three times, and had been unable to get within distance. I drove for them again, and, seeing that they were just going to fly, I pulled up and let go one barrel just as they rose. Of late years I have killed as many by driving for them with a smart horse as in any other way. When shooting in this method, I once killed five geese with the two barrels, and have often killed from ten to fifteen a day from the buggy. The greatest number I ever killed in a day was twenty-three. That was in a corn-field where the corn was in shock, and I shot from such a blind as I have described above. It was near Elkhart, and on one of those wet, misty days in the spring *on* which the Canada geese are flying about and feeding all day. I generally use No. 1 shot for geese. It is quite large enough with plenty of powder to drive it home. In shooting geese from a blind the shooter must keep quite still until they are near enough. When he has killed, he must pick up the goose and return to his blind.

When young wheat is among the corn-shocks, the small grain having been sown the previous fall, it is a favorite resort for wild geese. A live decoy—a wild goose that was winged, and which has been saved for the purpose—may be staked out in the field, and the geese will come down to it. In the fields of early spring wheat, where there are no corn-shocks, there are sometimes many geese. They eat off the green plants, and the farmers, thinking them an intolerable nuisance, used to put up scarecrows, as people do in some parts to keep away swamp blackbirds and crows from young springing corn. In such a wheat-field the shooter may dig a hole, and, smoothing over the ground, get into it and wait for the geese. If it is too wet for that, he may sink a large barrel or small hogshead, and from that get very nice shooting. From a barrel placed in a marsh known to be a good resort for geese, much shooting may be had all the spring season, but it must be planted there before the wild geese have come from the south. It is better than boat-shooting, and perhaps better than any other plan, taking the spring season all through. When a hole is dug in a' wheat-field to which the wild geese have taken, it should be made soon after their arrival; and when they get used to it, much nice shooting may be had there.

But the best shooting at Canada geese, and the best geese for the table, are in the fall of the year, when the young geese come on from the far northern regions in which they have been bred. Their arrival is not looked for until we have had some stiff frost, and that is usually about the first of November. The corn is then just being cut up, and the fall wheat is well out of the ground. At first the wild geese go upon the young wheat, and they eat it off close sometimes. When the corn has been shocked and left on the fields, they go into that. The various kinds of wild geese, ducks, and cranes consume a great deal of corn. In some wet places I have known them to eat a third of the crop. Later on in the winter the wild geese do not go into the standing corn, as wild ducks do. The former are equally wary and more shy, and they will not go into places where there seems to be afforded a chance to crawl on them. In regard to their roosting-places wild geese are cunning and secretive. They mostly choose for their sleeping-places large, wet marshes and the margins of ponds in big bottoms, where there is open water. When there is ice in the marshes and on the ponds, they roost on that. These roosting-places are generally far away from the settlements, and in places that are almost inaccessible. A few flocks still roost near the ponds in the Salt Creek and Sangamon bottoms. These bottoms are more than a mile wide in some places, and the bottoms of the Illinois and Mississippi Rivers are wider still. Crane Lake in Mason County, a wild, marshy place, is a favorite roost- ing-place for wild geese.

When a roosting-place has been found, capital success may be looked for. It can seldom be found except by watching the flights of wild geese nights and mornings, having a good knowledge of the country, and using proper judgment. The shooter goes to it at sundown, and, lying down inthe grass with clothes of the proper hue, waits for geese. They come in late in the evening, and keep coming, flock after flock, until nine or ten at night, and sometimes until eleven. On Mr. Sulli- vant's tract, in Ford County, before they are much shot at, the wild geese roost about the ponds in the prairie; but when they have been disturbed there a few times, they go further off to wild places in the extensive swamps. Wild geese do not frequent timber-land, except when the weather is very cold and blustering, or when there is a fall of snow. At those times they go into the timber along creeks and rivers, and may be found there.

Some years ago I and three others found out that there was a small roosting-place on the Sangamon River just below the mouth of Salt Creek. There came a sudden frost and intense cold weather, with some snow. We knew that at such a time the river would, be frozen over near the place the geese frequented, and that they would roost on the ice. At break of day we got up, and drove in a sleigh three miles to where we knew the wild geese would be found. In. such weather they do not fly before nine or ten o'clock in the morning. The river was low, and

before we got to the bank we could hear the flock of geese, on the ice below, chattering in the cold. There was heavy timber on both banks, and we crept up in it on our side until we were within about forty yards of the pack of geese on the ice below. As we raised ourselves up, the wild fowl started to fly, and we put in the discharge from, our eight barrels as they were rising, and killed ten. Our guns were muzzle-loaders. If they had been breech-loaders, we could have charged and shot again, as the geese seemed bewildered for a little while, and did not fly straight away. Now began my bad luck.

The wild geese, as a matter of course, fell on the ice. It was what is called slush ice, which is none of the strongest, but weak and treacherous even when thick. My companions were afraid to go out for the dead geese, and I had to go, though the heaviest man of the party. It is my habit, when out shooting, hardly ever to let my gun be out of my hands, and it was now lucky that in going on the ice for these geese l carried it with me. I had brought some of the geese to the bank, and gone out for the balance. The furthest two I got, and was just stooping to pick up the last when in I went.I had gone in a sort of air-hole, which, being covered with broken ice and snow, I had not pjerceived. The river was twenty feet deep, and I came near being drowned. However, by means of the gun in one hand and the three geese in the other, I got such a spread on the ice that I did not go clean under. Two of my companions were so scared by the suddenness of the occurrence and the danger of the situation that they could do nothing. The other got an old ten-foot rail, and, shoving it to me, enabled me to struggle to the bank, gun, geese, and all. The cold was so intense that my clothes were all frozen stiff the minute after I was out of the water. It was three miles to a house and a stove, and before we got there I was like a solid six-foot chunk of ice. I then got on dry clothes, wrapped myself in a blanket, took a seat by the fire, and drank half a pint of strong whiskey, neat. I was soon all right again; but when the blood began to circulate in the numbed parts, the pain, was intense for the time. I did not even take cold from that ducking.

Being much in the water, however, in the Western country, entails something worse than a cold, if not worse than .rheumatism. I mean the ague.

12

SECTION 12

When I first went to Illinois, I shot many geese; and if one feil in a pond or slough, I waded in waist-deep to bring it out. The old settlers used to tell me that it was a bad practice; but I had never been sick in my life to any degree of importance, and had no fears. But after being there a year, out in all sorts of weather, and often in and out of the water two or three times
   a day, I caught the ague, and had it eleven months. It was not the mild ague, such as prevails to some extent on the Atlantic coast of the Northern States, but the powerful Western ague, which shakes a man so that his bones almost rattle as well as his teeth. In the course of the eleven months it was broken up several times, but always came back again. Now, there are a great many *infallible* remedies for the ague. I took about a score of them, but didn't get well. At last, however, I got hold of the real thing. It cured me, and much experience of it since for sixteen years has convinced me that it is the best thing in the world to cure the complaint. It is not a patent medicine. The editor of this book, to whom I am relating my experience, and who had experience of the shakes himself in Michigan from July to Christmas, says he wishesit was, as ve could get five hundred dollars, in that case, for this notice of it. It is simply lemon-juice and Holland gin. Squeeze the juice of five or six lemons into a quart of gin, and take a good dram of it three times a day. It is not only pleasant, but effectual, and it will cure

as well as prevent the ague. At the same time avoid getting wet as much as possible, especially in the ponds and sloughs.

Shooting brant geese is much the same in method as shooting Canada geese. They are about half the size of the, latter, and very good eating. There is this difference in their habits: the brant do not go so much into fields where the corn is shocked, but use more where it is not cut up, but the stalks are much broken down. In the early spring a man may see acres of such corn-fields covered with brant. To shoot them there he must lie down as I have directed for duck- shooting in the like places. With .the brant, at least in close proximity, will be found what we call Mexican geese. They are about the same size as the brant, and though there are at least four kinds, to judge by the plumage and markings, they are in flocks all mixed up together. Sometimes there will be half a dozen brant in aflock of these mixed Mexicans. The latter are more numerous now than either Canada geese or brant. They have increased in number of late years, not only relatively, but absolutely. Just before they go off northwards in the spring the mixed flocks of these geese pack together on the prairies and on rather elevated spots until there are three or four thousand in a body. They leave in these great packs. When they have gathered, and are preparing to set out on their long flight they may be seen to rise and circle round so as to cast a shadow on the ground like a cloud. These geese fly by night. They always seem to arrive in the night, and they leave by night. They utter a different cry from Canada geese and from brant, and are much more noisy than either. When, in their flight through the air, they go over, or nearly over, the lights of a town or village, they make a great row. On the table they are plump and nice, as good as brant, but to my thinking not as good as the Canada goose. That is the king of the wild geese; more juicy than any other, as well as twice the size. The great mixed flocks of Mexican geese present a mottled appearance when clearly seen. Some are pale blue in color, some grizzly gray, some have whiteheads and nocks, some are all white except the ends of the wings, which in them are black. If any naturalist of New York, Boston, or Philadelphia would like to have a specimen of each of these geese, 1 can send them.

There are two kinds of cranes plentiful in Illinois in the spring and fall of the year. The most abundant is the sand-hill crane, a well-known bird. With a body as large as that of a goose, he stands upon long legs, so that he is four and a half or five feet high. They winter in the south, and go to high northern latitudes to breed. A few nests are made in the Winnebago Swamp, but only a few. They do not resort about water much, although they choose their roosting-place near it. In the spring they are first seen very high in the air, circling round and uttering loud cries, so high up as hardly to be perceived. In my opinion, they fly higher than any other bird, not even excepting eagles and vultures. When the cry of the crane is heard coming out of the sky, as it -were, people know that winter is quite over, and that warm weather is going to come in shortly. When seen sitting on the prairie in flocks, they look like sheep at a distance.

They arrive with us according to the season,
usually about the tenth of March, and stay a month. Like the wild geese and ducks, cranes frequent the corn-fields for the purpose of feeding. The few nests made in Illinois contain but two eggs, and one of the old birds is always on the watch near

them. They return in the fall about the same time as the wild geese, but do not then fly so high as in the spring; perhaps it is because many of them are young birds. In the fall they are first seen out on the prairie, and a very unwelcome sight it is to the farmer; for they are very hard on his crop of corn, much of which is then cut up and shocked in the fields. Boys are employed to keep them away. I have often seen large pieces of corn-land in shock when all the ears on the outside had been shelled and eaten, not a kernel left. They stay as long as the wild geese, which is until real hard weather sets in. Cranes are easy birds to shoot when you can get a fair shot at them, but they are wary and shy, keeping a good lookout all the time. It is of no use to lie down in corn for them. They can see further and better than any other bird I know. The immense height at which they fly in the spring has convinced me of this. To shoot them, when they have been shot at and made shy and wary, one of two methods must be fol-

lowed. By watching their flights to and from corn-fields their crossing-places may be found. At one of these the shooter must post himself under an Osage orange hedge on the windward side. Then he must wait for a lot to come over. In windy weather and going to windward they fly low and slow, and are very easily hit. But it takes hard hitting to kill them, as they are thickly feathered. When going for cranes, I use No. 1 or No. 2 shot in my cartridges with strong charge of powder. Some think heavier shot necessary, but I know they are not. At Mr. Sullivant's farm in Ford County, last spring, I shot twenty sand-hill cranes and three of the large white variety. I had no larger shot than No. 6, having gone without expectation of getting any shooting except at ducks, mallards, and pintails.

There were, however, large numbers of cranes, and I found out that they roosted near ponds in the neighboring prairie. I knew then that I could get close shots when they came at dusk. Loading my cartridges for that shooting with six drams of powder and an ounce of shot, and taking post near the edge of the pond, which was from one to two acres in extent, I waited for their coming. The first evening I killed seven sand-hill cranesand the three large white ones, and the next night thirteen of the sand-hills. The large white crane i-' lugger than the sand-hill, and sometimes attains the enormous weight of thirty pounds; that is, he weighs as much as two good turkeys. It is pure white, except the ends of the wings, which are Hack. The largest of the three I killed was a magnificent specimen. lie measured seven feet eight inches across the wings, stood five feet ten inches high, and weighed thirty pounds. I gave it to Mr. Gillott, of the great farm near Elkhart, and he had a description of it published in the Lincoln, Logan County, paper, headed, " Captain Bogardus's Mammoth Crane."

It is hard to get within shot of the white crane. They are seldom killed, except near the ponds, when they come to roost at night. It has a very keen as well as far sight, and nothing but the fact that it is almost dark when they come to the roosting-place enables the shooter to get a chance at them. A crane of either kind winged will make a desperate fight, and is a dangerous customer for the unwary to deal with. If man or dog comes within striking distance, the crane aims at the eye with his sharp-pointed bill, some six inches long. The bird will drive his bill into a dog asif it were a dagger. I have had a dog that had never seen crane before go in to catch one that was winged, but he came out again after getting one stroke. The white crane is not nearly as numerous as the sand-hill. Its habits are the same, but there are only from eight to twelve in a flock. I never saw a nest of this crane, and believe it never builds in Illinois.

Both the cranes are fine eating. The meat is dark, and the breast, when well hung and properly cooked, is as fine as the best venison. At one time I thought they were good for nothing, but a circumstance happened which changed my opinion altogether. I was out shooting pinnated grouse late in the fall with a companion, and we camped, or rather took shelter, slept, and cooked in a herdsman's hut which had been deserted. The cattle had been driven away, and the hut was tenant- less. It was on the Delavan prairie. I killed a sand-hill crane, and hung it on the fence by the hut. It remained there eight or nine days and as many frosty nights. We had good sport, plenty to eat, and forgot all about the crane. But on the evening of one day, on which, we had sent all our game away in the afternoon, it was found that by an oversight we had reserved nonefor our suppers and breakfasts. I then remembered the crane, and going to the fence I picked the breast, and cut it off in slices or steaks. These we fried. in butter. There was a prairie road or track running by the hut. It was commonly but little used, but on this occasion, while the steaks were being cooked, a man and a woman came by in a buggy. As she caught the rich flavor from the hot pan, the woman said, "Those men must have something very good to eat." She was right. When we came to our crane-steaks, we both thought we had never eaten anything so good in our lives. It is true that the frosty air of the prairie late in the fall sharpens the appetite, and true that we were hungry, and hunters at that; but it is also true that the steaks were delicious eating. The meat was rich and juicy, and it had been frozen and thawed a sufficient number of times to make it very tender. Since then, if a crane was within shot, I have never let him get away, if I could help it. The flesh of the white crane is quite as good as that of the sand-hill kind. .

Cranes need to be hung for a long time before being cooked, and almost all game is the better for being hung, if the weather is cool orcold. Perhaps snipe and woodcock may be exceptions. You can hardly hang pinnated grouse too long when they keep sweet. I have eaten them a month after they were killed in the winter, and none could be finer. Quail are all the better for being hung. So are Canada geese and other wild geese, together with mallard ducks and wild turkeys. Of course young grouse shot in August or the warm days of September cannot be hung, and they are very good eating when cooked fresh, but not better than winter grouse)iung a long time, stuffed, roasted, and eaten with bread-sauce, made gravy, and hot, mealy potatoes.

A few pelicans are shot along the upper part of the Mississippi River. Occasionally a small flight of swans come over Central Illinois, and sometimes they alight in the Winnebago Swamp or the Sangamon bottoms; but these occurrences are rare. My brother once killed three late in the fall on the Sangamon bottom. They were going south, and alighted at a pond where he was lying for geese at roosting-time. At a place in the Winnebago Swamp called Swan Lake they sometimes alight on their passage. I have never killed one. Going down the Mississippi last winter, I saw, from the steamboat, many swans inthe bayous and on the sand-islands. At New Orleans I was told by Mr. Charleville, the gunsmith, that there was a fine place for shooting all sorts of wild fowl below the city, called The Dump. I saw plenty of mallards, there called French ducks, in the market

CHAPTER XIII.
WILD TURKEY AND DEER SHOOTING.

Of all the feathered game that runs and flies, the wild turkey of America is the noblest and most beautiful of which I ever heard. In one sense the ostrich of the Arabian desert or the emu of the Australian plains might be deemed an exception. They, however, do not fly; and though their size, plumage, and fleetness invest them with a sort of grandeur, and their feathers are valuable as ornaments for the head-dresses of ladies, they are neither so beautiful nor so useful and excellent as food as the wild turkey. Indeed, the flesh of the latter is hardly surpassed by anything in succulence, richness of flavor, and nutriment, and it is vastly superior to that of any tame turkey that ever was fed and roasted or boiled. It is well known that the tame turkey is descended from the wild turkey of America. Before the discovery of this continent the bird was unknown in Europe, and had never been seen in Turkey in Asia. It may be easily domesticated,and a cross of the wild gobbler with tame hen- turkeys always improves the flock in size and excellence.

At one time the wild turkey was plentiful all over this country, from Texas to Canada, and from the eastern seaboard to the peaks of the Rocky Mountains, in such localities as furnished it with its favorite sorts of food and afforded the cover in which it delights. Now, however, it is hardly to be met with to the eastward of West Virginia, and it cannot be said to be still abundant in Ohio, Kentucky, Indiana, Michigan, Illinois, etc. In those States wild turkeys were once very plentiful, and a considerable number are still to be found in a few localities in each. In Iowa, Missouri, etc., there are more wild turkeys now than in the States first mentioned. One would suppose there must still be a few in the western parts of New York and Pennsylvania, but I am not certain that there are.

Tlia wild turkey is a bird of the forest rather than of the prairies or the plains. It makes its haunts in timber-land, large pieces of woods, and groves, and betakes itself to thick brush and the neighborhood of impassable swamps to breed. It comes out, however, at night or at earliest dawn,and feeds in the corn and wheat fields in the fall, and many broods are sometimes seen together in a pack a hundred strong, led by old gobblers. In the beech and maple woods it feeds upon beechnuts with great relish, and, indeed, its principal food in winter is the berries of the bushes and the " mast" of various trees. The wild turkey, though so gregarious, is shy and a wary, fast- running bird, hardly ever taking to the wing if it can avoid doing so. When closely pursued by a dog or impeded by deep snow, it is compelled to flight.

It is found in Illinois in the timber and thick brush to be met with on the banks of rivers and creeks. The wild turkeys used to be very numerous in and about the bottoms of the Sangamon River. I have killed a great many there myself, one of which was a famous gobbler of twenty- seven pounds weight and magnificent plumage. They are now scarce, difficult to find, and hard to kill. Following turkeys on their tracks in snow, which has been rny usual method of hunting them, is hard work. In the great woods of the forest countries the favorite method is to find the flock, scatter it all around by means of a dog, and then in ambush imitate the call of the turkeysuntil they come near enough to be shot with a rifle.

There used to be many turkeys in the timber at Lake Fort, some seven or eight miles from Elkhart, and a few may be found there yet. In the. woodlands of North Missouri the wild turkey is still rather abundant, and it will be found wherever there is timber and brush all through Missouri, Kansas, Arkansas, the Indian Territory, and down through Texas. Wild turkeys are also found in Louisiana, Alabama, Georgia, and Florida. They do best in warm weather, though they are furnished with a full coat of feathers, and can stand the cold of our northwestern States and Canada.

I have often found the wild turkey's nest. It is made in the timber, among thick brush, and very often by the side of an old log. When the hen wild turkey leaves her nest, she covers it up with leaves, just as the tame hen-turkey will do when she has made a nest under a hedge or in the brambles near a fence. Some years ago, when wild turkeys abounded more than they do now, great numbers of their eggs were taken from their nests and hatched under hens. The young ones thus obtained were verymuch like young tamo turkeys in their-habits until late in the fall. Then, from roosting in trees and rambling about, they often left the tame turkeys, and went off with the wild ones. In secluded places the wild turkeys often mingle with tame flocks. The gobblers are not pugnacious with each other, though they will fight with game-cocks, and sometimes, by superior weight and strength, worry out and kill the best.

Formerly I used to shoot turkeys in the old method of calling them up, after having scattered them, to an ambush, and using a smallbore rifle or a shot-gun loaded with buckshot or with BB cartridge. That plan answers best when the turkeys are young. Latterly I have waited for turkey-shooting until the winter weather had well set in, and gone only when there was snow on the ground. The method is to find the tracks of a flock in the snow, and follow them up. Turkeys in snow, with a man following in their track, soon begin to tire a little, if the snow is damp and no crust on the top of it. After some time the hunter, who must be a good walker and capable of standing much fatigue, will see where one of the turkeys has diverged from the route of the flock. Following the trackof the single turkey, it will be found that after having gone a little way, commonly not more than two hundred yards, and often less, it has squatted under thick brush or in the top of a fallen tree. As he draws near, it will start to run or to fly, and it must then be shot. In this sport I use No. 1 shot, which is quite big enough. A turkey going to fly is compelled to run eight or ten feet in order to get headway before rising from the ground, and I have often shot them in the head before they could take wing. After having killed his turkey, the hunter must take up the track of the flock again, and go on after it until he sees that another has diverged. As I remarked before, it is much the best to follow this sport when the snow is damp, for the turkeys then tire the sooner, and are more inclined to hide and squat. No dog is to be used. He would be worse than useless.

Another good time for turkey-shooting is when it is snowing hard. That, of course, is no good time for tracking; but while the snow is falling fast, the wild turkeys sit around in thick brush or in the thick top of a fallen tree. They are then easily approached ; but the hunter must know the country well, and be familiar withthe places where the flocks habitually resort. If the hunter does not know the country well, and is after turkeys in a thick snow-storm, instead of finding them, he will be likely enough to get lost himself.

When a flock of wild turkeys is being followed by tracking, they often take wing; and there, of course, their tracks end. But they generally fly straight ahead, and the hunter may usually hit their new tracks after they have alighted and gone on again on foot. Although they fly straight, they do not travel straight when on foot, but sometimes wind in and out very much. Commonly their tracks will be found again within three or four hundred yards of where they took wing. The hunter will see where they made the quick run before rising. By that he may judge very nearly the direction of their flight, and follow it.

When there are creeks and ravines which turkeys must cross on the wing, they almost always go over at the same places. In such a case as a creek running across a narrow belt of timber, or a ravine intersecting it, advantage may be taken of this habit of the turkeys. There must be two hunters. One must post himself at the crossing under cover, and the other go three or four miles up, and drive the wood down to it. If there are any turkeys in the upper part of the timber, the man at the crossing will be certain to have a good shot or two.

When I first lived in Illinois, I used to hunt turkeys a good deal on the Sangamon, in the right kind of weather, generally preferring soft snow or a fast-falling snow-storm. I generally killed some turkeys|some days only two, on others three, four, five, and six, and a few times as many as seven. One day I was tracking turkeys in only about three inches of snow. They did not tire, but travelled fast, and sometimes took flight, so that following them was a weary business. I had been after them nearly all day, and was nearly " tuckered out." I had often been in sight of them, but never near enough for a shot. But as evening drew on apace, and roosting-time approached, the turkeys began to call. They had travelled all day, and were glad to halt where they were. By waiting and stalking between calls I shot four. They weighed from twelve to eighteen pounds each, and I had to carry them and my gun three miles to get to a house. It was a very hard day's work, and nothing but downright perseverance enabled me to get any turkeys at all on that occasion. When the going is good, a flock of turkeys will beat a man by endurance. They are great ramblers in the daytime, -but nearly always come back to the same roosting- place at night.

On another occasion I was out after turkeys ' a the Sangamon on a thick, snowy day|just the sort of day for a man to get lost in timber and a wild, broken country. I then lived seven miles from Petersburg, and in following the turkeys round bluffs and across barrens on the edge of the timber I was several times in sight of that place. Still the tracks went on winding about until they led to a place where there seemed to be some every way. There were others besides myself hunting turkeys in that timber, and we sometimes took the tracks ahead of each other. It was then snowing rather fast, and of course the tracks were all fresh. The flock I was on tired in the afternoon, and I killed two about four o'clock. I then found I was lost. It was still snowing, and night was coming on. The first thing to be done was to keep on as fast as I could in one direction, so as to get out of the timber. The turkeys I had killed were very large ones |twenty pounds each. However, I trudged along through the snow, and at last got clear of the woods, and found out where I was. It was not, however, as I had expected, between Petersburg and where I lived, but at Indian Point, from which I had a walk of thirteen miles home. I do not think I ever was more tired than I was that night when

I reached home. Travelling in snow is not easy walking, and tracking turkeys in it is emphatically hard work.

I went out one day to hunt wild turkeys near the mouth of Salt Creek in seven or eight inches of wet snow, the weather being mild and the frost giving, so that the snow packed. I came upon the tracks of a flock of turkeys, and, after following them for some time, I killed two. Taking up the main trail again, I noticed the track of one very large turkey, a real great gobbler. I had heard other men speak of having been on the track of a very large turkey about there, but none of them had ever been able to come up with him, though they had killed others out of the flock he led. I now determined to do my best to get him, and resolved not to go off after stragglers,unless he left the route of the flock himself. 1 followed the track, winding through brush, and sometimes went across very rough ground|over which the turkeys flew|for as much as ten miles; but in the timber of the bottom I was unable to come up to the gobbler. The other turkeys in the flock appeared to have straggled ofF, and the old, wily gobbler, often hunted and very fast, and strong as well as large, was alone. At last he left the bottoms, and the trail led up into bluffs and ravines where the brush was very thick and the snow in places quite deep. I think many men would have given it up then, for the ground was extremely difficult to enter into after the ten-mile tramp from where I had struck the trail first, but I determined to persevere. In fact, I had now strong .hopes of getting the turkey, being convinced that he would not have entered this ground if he had not been tired. After going some distance among the bluffs and thickets of the ravines, the gobbler squatted under an old tree-top. He would be dead beat and want rest sorely before he would do that, I knew; still, I looked for him to appear at any moment from some such place, and kept my gun ready, both locks cocked. He would get wind again while Iwas coming up on his track, and be ready for a quick bolt. As 1 advanced oil the trail, I heaid a movement among the top brush of a fallen tree, and out went the turkey. He was probably sixty yards away from me when I saw him so as to shoot, but I took a long shot, and hit him hard with the right barrel, following it with the left instanter to make sure work. I think the first barrel would have been enough, but I was very anxious to get him; and as 1 knew that if he was only winged he would run ur.til he dropped dead, I gave him the second barrel. He was the most splendid specimen of the wild turkey I ever saw, and I have seen a great many. He weighed twenty-seven pounds, was quite fat, and the beard|the tuft of hair which hangs from the breast|was eight inches long. The beauty of his plumage on the neck, wings, and breast is indescribable. It glittered with a score of hues of metallic lustre|gold, green, purple, brown, etc.| and these tints cast rays like those which flash from the feathers of the humming-bird.

It was *in* the belt of timber in which this gobbler was found that I then lived. On two occasions there I shot at a turkey on the wing with a rifle, when out after deer, and killed.When turkeys are too wild to be shot with a shot-gun, it is of little use to track them at all. Resort must then bo had to the method of calling them up, and here the rifle may be used. Except for very long shots, however, the shotgun is as good as the rifle, even when the turkeys are called up within distance of the shooter, and in one important matter better|there are two barrels to one, and a miss may be mended with the second.

The best day of turkey-shooting I ever had was in Missouri, on Shoal Creek, not a great distance from the town of St. Jo, on the Missouri River. I went to that quarter on a regular shooting expedition, prepared to stay some time. John D. Lindsay, an old hunter, went first in order to look about the neighborhood around St. Jo, and ascertain what the prospects were. He wrote to me that there were plenty of wild turkeys, deer, and other game in the region round about Cameron, Lynn County, and desired me to join him. I Jost no time in doing so, and was accompanied by Colonel Roberts, who wanted to camp out. We took my tent. Arriving at Cameron in the morning, I hired a team. We took the tent and other things out to a suitable spot about three or four miles fromthe town, and there prepared to camp. We pitched our tent on a creek bottom, near enough to the bank to make it handy to get water, and at the foot of a hill covered with scrub-oak. In selecting a place for a camp in cold weather the main things to look after are shelter from the northwest winds and close proximity to wood and water. I had no camp-stove then, and it was necessary to keep up a big fire near the mouth of the tent all night, so that plenty . of wood was required. The country for miles around was successive hills and hollows, with scrub-timber in places and much brush, called barrens. Having pitched the tent and plied our axes for wood, Lindsay and I left Colonel Roberts to put things to rights, took our guns, and went to look about a little. In less than half an hour I killed two turkeys. This was a good beginning.

We returned to the tent, where Colonel Eoberts speedily distinguished himself as a capital cook. Having picked and cleaned a turkey, he desired me to put up two short stakes with forks at the upper ends pretty close to the fire, while Lindsay was required to furnish a thin, straight stick. With this last the colonel spitted the turkey, andthe ends of the spit being laid in the crutches of the uprights, the bird could be turned slowly before the fire with little trouble. A pan placed beneath caught the gravy and dripping, and with this the turkey was basted from time to time. It was a most excellent roast, and a wild turkey cooked in this way before a big, quick fire beats one that is baked in an oven all hollow. We feasted well that evening, but in the night we rather suffered, as I shall relate.

We had to rely on a large fire in front of the .tent for warmth, as I had then no tent-stove. Of late years I have always been provided with a small, cheap stove and pipe, which could be put up inside. The tent being then closed all round, and a small fire kept up in the stove with hard wood, it is as warm inside as in a house. Such a plan is much better for convenience and comfort than my old system. The fire in front of the tent has to be eight or ten feet off, for fear that the canvas may take fire if it is nearer, and on a cold night it does not do much good. In Missouri at that time the nights were very cold. We had to lie with our heads under the blankets to keep our ears from being frozen. In the morning our boots were as stiff as if they had been made of iron instead of leather. We hunted every day with more or less success..

In a few days there came a fresh fall of snow, some seven or eight inches, and Lindsay and I went out prepared to take advantage of it. We breakfasted at break of day, and set out for Shoal Creek, which was three miles distant. It quit snowing as soon as it got to be daylight, so that when we reached the banks of the creek the tracks, if any were found, would be fresh. About eight o'clock in the morning we came upon the trail of a large flock of turkeys. They had begun to move about as soon as it left off snowing, and there must have been from thirty-five to forty, perhaps more than forty, in the flock. After following the track for a while I got sight of the flock, crept up within distance, and killed two, one with each barrel. The turkeys thereupon scattered and flew, and some passing near Lindsay, he killed one on the wing. Neither of us shot with a rifle. Those turkeys had not been shot at much, and they were nothing like as wild as those of Illinois. It was the best turkey-shooting I ever saw. We followed up the main body, and every now and then I would go after a straggler who had left it, and shoot him as he lefthis squatting-place. At noon 1 had killed eleven turkeys and Lindsay three. I got the most shots, as I went after the stragglers, while he kept on the track of the flock. The turkeys weighed from ten to eighteen pounds each. They were not quite so fat as our Illinois turkeys commonly are, but their flavor was delicious, and their flesh very tender and juicy|just what that of a wild turkey in perfection is.

We placed our turkeys safe hung in a tree, and, going to a house, got dinner, arranging with the man that he should take us and our game to our camp in the evening with his wagon and team. Deer were plentiful thereabout. In the afternoon I shot at a big buck with turkey- shot, and hit him hard. He bled freely as he ran, and we -followed on his trail. That prevented us from getting any more turkeys that day. We kept on the buck's track for a long distance, hoping to get another shot at him. We could not do so, however, and the trail finally led to a place where there had been such a number of deer that day that their tracks were all mixed up. We saw three going over the brow of a hill, but they were far out of shot. So we concluded to give up further exertions, and, returning to the house, we found the man and his team ready. On our road to camp we took up our turkeys, and ended a busy day with a capital supper by the blazing fire. It was the best day's turkey-shooting I ever had, and we could have got more of them if we had not been led off on a fruitless" chase after the deer. With breech-loading guns and buckshot cartridges in the left barrels for deer, we could have got several fat ones, as well as the turkeys.

In the three weeks we were in camp at Shoal Creek we shot between fifty and sixty turkeys, not going for them especially, except on favorable days, when fresh snow had fallen. Our sport in this neighborhood was good in every respect, but in one regard we had great discomfort. The weather was hard, and we were very cold at night. Young sportsmen will sometimes read descriptions in which the writers say that they slept out all night without a tent, the thermometer below zero, and that wrapped in their blankets, with their feet to the fire, they were very comfortable. In my opinion this is all humbug. I have been out many a night, but it was in , moderately warm weather.

The thing to be most apprehensive about then is a thunder-storm.

I was once caught in one in the middle of the night, early in the fall, on the Delavan Prairie, which is in Logan County, sixteen miles from Elkhart. The unbroken prairie was then eight or ten miles in extent. In fact, there was no cultivated land on it, except near the strips of timber by which it was bounded. I went out in a buggy, and alone, to shoot pinnated grouse in the evening, and though I meant to stay on the prairie all night, and shoot again in the morning, I took no tent. A blanket to lay on the ground under the buggy, and another to cover me, were deemed sufficient.

I shot until dark over two good dogs, and had fine sport. I then drove to a part of the prairie where men had been cutting grass for fodder, and left it in cocks, and pulled up there for the night. I tied the horse to the wheel, gave him a feed of corn in the bottom of the buggy, watered him, and tossed him down a lot of the new-made prairie-hay. The scent of it pervaded the air of the space all around, and was very sweet and grateful. I got my own cold supper, and, lying down under the buggy with the dog near me, I soon fell asleep. It was a still night, no air stirring even on the open prairie where I was when I went to rest. But about one o'clock there arose a strong wind, the forerunner of a mighty storm:

Awakened by the change in the weather, I got up, and, looking to windward, saw an immense black cloud looming high up towards the zenith, and coming on at a rapid rate towards the prairie. Knowing very well what it meant, and seeing the forked lightning already darting down from it, while the rumble of the distant thunder overbore the rushing of the wind, I piled up a lot of hay around the buggy to windward, and got under it again. I had not been there many minutes when the storm burst with fearful fury, seemingly right over my head. Then came lightning, thunder, and torrents of rain altogether, as it were. The lightning was so vivid and so rapid that the horse got scared and trembled, the dogs cowered and crept closer to me, and I was much alarmed. The lightning ran round the tires of the wheels, so that the wagon seemed to be shod with fire. It lit up the prairie at every flash, and the flashes were almost continuous, so that I could see white houses five or six miles off as plain, or plainer, than I could by day. The thunder-claps were so heavy that it appeared as if they would split my head open. For more than an hour the storm kept on. Then it abated almost as suddenly as it came, and I soon went to sleep again. This was the heaviest thunder-storm I ever experienced. 1 was more iu fear during that hour than 1 ever was before, or than I have been since. What with the horse and the dogs and myself altogether in a group, the bright tires of the wheels, and the steel locks and barrels of my gun, the danger must have been great. But, blessed be God, it was averted !

In the morning the dogs rose refreshed, as I did myself. They worked well. The scent lay thick on the wet ground, and I .never shot better. I killed forty-three grouse before the sun got very high in the forenoon, and returned home with a large bag of very fine birds.

When men camp out with a tent without a stove, and they keep a large fire in front of the tent, as they will be sure to do in cold weather, there is considerable danger that their canvas may take fire. I have had three tents burned up. A change of wind during the night may blow glowing embers right up to the canvas, and set fire to it, if no one is awake to look after it. And twice my tent caught fire in the daytime, when we thought there was no danger, and went off hunting with no one left at camp. Therefore I say to every one who means to camp out on sporting excursions, get a nice little stove. The cost is small, the comfort large, and, except through gross carelessness, there can be no danger whatever.

To give a description of the common deer of this country would be mere folly and impertinence. It is often supposed that it likes best to range in the vast forests, but I believe that to be a mistake. Deer are most fond of a country in which there are belts of timber-land and brush interspersed with prairies and savannas. Much of that part of Illinois where I lived at first is somewhat of that character. When I first went to the State, deer were exceedingly plentiful. I have myself seen as many as thirty in a herd, and men who had lived a long time an that part of Illinois, when I went to reside there, told me they had seen herds which could not have contained less than seventy-five. In the cold weather the deer went to the timber for shelter. In the warm weather they did not go much to the woodlandto pass the heat of the day, as one might have well supposed they would, but they spent some hours before and after noonday lying in the long grass of the prairie near sloughs, where it grows particularly rank and tall.

Deer have much decreased in number in that part of Illinois of late years, though they may still be met with occasionally, and shot by a man who knows how to go about it. In the earlier times of my residence in the State they used to feed upon the young wheat, where fall wheat had been sowed out upon the prairie. At about sunrise they might be seen feeding in these fields, and looking like so many calves. When it was broad daylight, they retired to the long grass near the sloughs, or to thick brush in the woodland, or to patches of high weeds, and there they would lie until evening. There are some deer in Ford County yet. Three or four were killed there last winter|two of them on Mr. Sullivant's farm. Another was chased right through the town of Gibson, and killed below it. At Oliver's Grove, in Iroquois County, there used to be largo numbers of deer, and some may be found there yet. In the southern part of Illinois, down toward and in the district called Egypt, deer are found infair numbers. But the best place near Illinois in which to hunt them i8 the northern part of Missouri. Deer are numerous in parts of Kansas, and about Omaha, Nebraska, there are many to be found.

This last-named city is a good point for sporting tourists ; various descriptions of game abound, and the shooting club includes many excellent sportsmen and gentlemen among its members. The best place in the city to obtain information as to localities and to meet sportsmen is the store of Mr. D. C. Sutphen, gunmaker and dealer. And a very good place to stop at, as I found by personal experience, is the Grand Central Hotel. Wild turkeys, deer, pinnated grouse, wild geese, ducks, etc., may be shot in the vicinity of Omaha.

The first deer I ever killed was in Woodford County, Illinois. I was out with an old hunter, who set me to follow the track of the herd, and took post himself at a runway, where he thought he should be sure to get a good shot. But it did not so fall out. I followed a herd of five or six for about three miles, and on coming to the top of a hill I saw a deer in the valley below, standing on the edge of the slope, with its side to me. He was about two hundred yards off, but I determined to have a crack at him, and, throwing my rifle up, 1 took aim just behind the lower part of the shoulder. Mine was an old-fashioned, long, hunting-rifle, with steel barrel, carrying a ball forty to the pound. At the shot the deer made a buck-jump full ten feet into the air, and bounded away. I thought 1 had missed him, but my partner, on coming to the spot where he had stood, and looking narrowly around, thought not, and determined to follow his tracks. The fact was, as he told mo soon afterwards, that he saw a tinge of blood upon the snow on the other side of% the place where the deer had stood when I shot at him, and concluded that the ball had gone through him. He soon found that the deer straddled in his tracks and spread his hoofs, and then ho knew he was badly wounded.

The buck was found dead two hundred yards from where he was when 1 shot at him. The ball had gone clean through him, and also through his heart, after which he ran two hundred yards. I did not hunt deer much at that time, but I was soon a good shot with the rifle, and have killed a running deer with it.

I afterwards became acquainted with a mannamed Wilcox, who was the greatest deer-hunter in Illinois. lie had a system of his own, and a very successful system it certainly was, as he managed it. He hunted on horseback, and his weapon was a heavy double-barrelled shot-gun, with strong charges of powder and buckshot. Late in the fall, when the sloughs were low and held but little water, he used to ride down the middle .of them. When a deer got up from among the long grass on either side, Wilcox fired from the back of the horse, and knocked the buck or doe over. I soon found that was the best way, and adopted it myself, but I never had as much success at it as Wilcox did. The trouble was that 1 could neither get a really steady horse under fire nor. shoot very well on horseback at that time. The horse Wilcox used in his hunts had been accustomed to it so long that he knew just what was wanted, and when the reins were dropped he stood like a rock until the gun went off.

When deer are lying down, it is much easier to approach their lair, so as to get a shot on their rising, on horseback than on foot. It is now obsolete in our part of Illinois, as there arc no deer to shoot; but I should think it might be followedto advantage in Alabama, Louisiana, Texas, and Arkansas, where there are still plenty. It should also be tried in Missouri, Kansas, Nebraska, etc. Even in barrens and timber-land it would be better to hunt deer in this way than to still hunt for them on foot, if the ground is practicable for a horse. In some rugged places a horse cannot go; and in wet marshes, morasses, and shaking bogs a horse with a man on his back would sink in and be unable to struggle out. In Missouri deer are generally driven with hounds, and shot at crossing-places and runways. There are also many killed by still hunting.

To have any chance of success in deer-hunting, it is necessary that the sportsman should know the lay of the country and the places in which they are likely to be found. A stranger to the neighborhood had better get an old hunter to go out with him for a few days. A knowledge of their habits in the different localities is required, and it would take a long time to learn these if they were not imparted by some one who knows them. The deer are now wild and shy in most places. They have a keen nose, and can scent a man to windward before he can see them, which makes it requisite to hunt up-wind.Some deer are shot at salt-licks, to which they resort at night, and I believe the practice of fire- hunting is sometimes followed in the south. It is not pursued in the West.

13

SECTION 13

CHAPTER XIV.
THE ART OF SHOOTING ON THE WING.

The practical art of shooting birds on the wing, valuable accomplishment as it is, delightful in itself, and highly conducive to health and strength by leading to vigorous exercise in the fields, is readily acquired. Any one who is well enough to walk abroad and carry a gun may attain fair proficiency in it; for those whose nervous temperament prevents this are few indeed, and need not be taken into account. Some men, indeed, have a natural gift, by means of which, with the great practice such gift and its corresponding inclination are sure to induce, they become dead shots, the masters of the art of shooting. Still, there are very few who may not become good shots if they follow proper methods and practice much in pursuance of wise instructions. To begin at an early age is a good thing. Many boys can shoot as well as men, allowing for the smaller practice and shorter experience they have had. The parents of some youths are disinclined to let them have

guns for fear of accidents, but there is no ground for apprehension on this point. The handling of the gun prevents accidents with guns, instead of causing them. In those cases we hear of in which thoughtless persons shoot their friends accidentally, it will be found in nineteen cases out of twenty that the gun was not in the hands of a

Field, Cover, and Trap Shooting. Adam H. Bogardus

boy or young man who shoots in the field, but in those . of one who only knows a gun by sight, and is wholly unacquainted with the proper management of it. It is a million to one that a boy who shoots, or is learning to shoot, will never shoot one of his sisters or friends. Such things are only done by those who have nothing to do with firearms in their proper places. The latter have an idea that they will kill, but they hardly know how. On the other hand, the shooter sees execution done by his gun on birds, and, knowing that there is death in the barrel, never fools about with it, letting the muzzle cover people. Therefore I say that wherever there is convenience for it parents should let their sons learn to shoot, and they need not be afraid to do so because their boys are comparatively young. There is no more danger of a gun, to himself or other persons, in the hands of a boy of fourteen years of age, than there is ofone in the hands of a young man of twenty who is equally new to the practice of shooting. The boys must begin some time, if they are to shoot at all, and to put it off reminds one of the mother who declared that her son must not go into the water until he had learned to swim.

I now purpose to give such brief instructions to beginners in shooting and young sportsmen, together with hints which may be taken advantage of by marksmen of experience, as I believe will be useful. Two of the things essential to success in the field are the loading of the gun for the different varieties of game, and its handling when game is found and takes wing. It is a common error to use shot of a size larger than necessary, and very often there is too much of it. A timid man is afraid to put in plenty of powder, of which there can hardly be too much as long as the gun will burn it, and he increases the charge of shot under the strange delusion that he thus compensates for the deficiency of the explosive part of the charge. A gun badly loaded is like a bad watchlit deceives and mortifies its owner.

The choice of guns has been already alluded to, and, I repeat, beware of choosing one that is

very light. In a gun of more weight the capa- city of shooting strong charges with ease and comfort, and of killing more game, altogether outweighs the carrying of an extra pound or pound and a half. Boys, it is true, must have light guns, and there are very nice, safe, good-shooting guns made for boys. In choosing one for your son or nephew, however, do not choose a light gun of those made for boys. It is not to be a sort of handsome toy-gun, but a serviceable article, such as will inspire the boy with the confidence which -begets success and leads to skill, by hitting and killing whenever it is held right. The light single-barrelled guns made for boys do not amount to much. It will be better, in buying a gun for a youth who has not had one before, to pay more money and purchase a breech-loader, single-barrel if he is young and not strong, but a double-barrel if he is fifteen years old and fairly robust. Generally the height of the youth is not to be taken into account in this matter. Many boys who are not tall for their age have more strength and endurance than those who are. A breech-loader is much more easily loaded and a great deal safer than a muzzle-loader, as regards accidents, in the hands of either man or boy.

The gun being provided, the youth to whom it belongs is to handle it, and practise the handling of it, just as if it was loaded, until he brings it up to his shoulder clean and well, and feels as well able to manage it nicely and quickly as he is to handle his bat at base-ball or cricket. In this practice with the gun he is to be careful that he never lets the muzzle look towards a person. It is to be a cardinal principle that the gun in his hands, whether charged or not, shall never point towards man or boy, woman or girl, in the field, or the house, or anywhere else. When the youth handles the gun well unloaded, the next thing is to load. Young sportsmen in embryo must begin with light charges. For a breech-loader he may use the metal cases for his cartridges, or the paper cases if he does not want to use the case more than once. The gun-maker will show him how to load them, and until he can do it properly himself he had better get it done by a friend who understands it. He will learn to do it very easily.

At first the cartridges for the youth or young man must be loaded lightly; for if they are not, and his gun should kick, he may become afraid of it, shut both his eyes when he pullstrigger, hold it unsteadily, and fall into such habits as may prevent him from ever becoming a good shot. He will already have learned to stand upright, with his left foot in advance, and his right a little' back to brace the body when he brings his gun up as if to deliver fire.

With cartridges loaded with three or three and a half drachms of powder and an ounce of shot, No. 8 or No. 9, the youth is to go into a field, yard, or any safe place, and put up a target of paper a foot square against a building, a wall, a tree, or a board. He may then retire twenty yards, load his gun, take aim right along the rib of a double-barrel, along the top of the barrel and sight if single, and as soon as he has taken aim pull the trigger. I think a boy will usually get a quicker and better sight with a double- barrel gun than with a single-barrel. In taking aim the youth will naturally shut his left eye, and this is proper. I have heard men say that it is best to shoot without shutting one eye. For my part 1 cannot see it. One eye is certainly quite as good as two when it is taking aim along the gun at the object, and I believe a good deal better. In snap-shooting both eyes are often open when the fire is delivered, but even inthat most good shots instinctively shut the left eye at the instant of firing.

The youth must load again after his shot, and then go up to the target to see how many shot he put into it, change the paper, and try again. The main points are to get good, quick aim, and then fire on the instant, with the gun firmly held and well braced against the shoulder. But the gun is not to be fired in a hurried, hap-ha- zard sort of way without a sight being obtained at all. When the object is once sighted, the shooter is to fire, and not delay the discharge under the notion that he can do better. The first sight is the best. With practice and the consumption of a little powder and shot the youth will soon become familiar with the shooting of his gun, and learn to bring it up, take aim, and fire without any pause between those operations. He will then find that he can hit the target every time with the centre of the charge; and as this is the way to kill, he is now to begin at birds. Boys have a hankering after shooting at sitting birds. This is not to be indulged in. The target is better practice than sitting birds, because if the youthful shooter goes after the latter he will ramble about half a day without getting asmany shots in distance as he can make at the target in a quarter of an hour. Therefore, -when the young shooter begins at birds, it is to be at birds on the wing|slow-flying birds, such as meadow-larks, swamp blackbirds, and the like.

The young shooter will be able to get within twenty yards of larks. When the bird gets up, bring the gun to the shoulder, take quick aim, and fire. There is to be no dwelling on the aim, which is to be point blank at a bird going straight away from the gun, just as the sight was plump on the target. By going into the meadows and fields where swamp blackbirds fly up and down, the young sportsman may stand and shoot at them as they go by. These will be cross-shotslor side shots, as I call them, because the side of the bird is presented to the gun. One bird must always be selected for the shot, when there is a flock, or several birds arc flying near together; and as the course of the bird is across the line of fire, allowance must be made for that fact. The aim must be a little ahead of the flying bird. At short distances and at slow-flying birds a little is enough, but there should be some allowance made. For these birds at short distances No. 10 shot will bo large

14

SECTION 14

enough. When longer shots arc in order for the improving shooter, No. 8 may be used; and as he will now have acquired confidence in himself and his gun, more powder may be employed. After a while he will learn the quantity of powder with which his gun shoots best with ease and comfort to himself in delivering fire.

At first the young shooter at birds on the wing may expect misses, perhaps a good many of them, but he need not be disheartened. When he misses, let him consider and hit upon the probable cause of the miss. It may be that he shot too high or too low, or behind the bird|which is very likely if it was a cross-shot|or he may have shot in a hurried, flustered way without taking aim. To whatever cause he thinks the miss may have been owing, let him resolve to guard against it another time. 1 wish to impress upon the young shooter that missing within easy distance is not a matter of chance. Under such circumstances there is always a cause why the miss was not a hit, and it is desirable that he who has made it should find out the cause and be prepared to prevent it. If he does this, he will steadily improve in his shooting, and may probably become in time a " crack shot," whichsignifies one of the best. Going on missing time after time, without stopping to consider why the bird was missed, will not do.

When a bird is going straight away from the gun, the miss of the beginner is commonly owing to under-shooting. His line of fire, straight ahead, is apt to be correct, but he often shoots too low. Let him remember that a bird getting up near him and flying away is almost always rising for some distance. If the young shooter gets sight of the bird, he is certain not to shoot too high, and he may shoot too low; therefore keep the gun up, and if you see a feather of the bird in sighting along the ridge, crack away. You will be nearly certain to bring it down. Misses at birds which present side shots, and fly across the line of fire, are usually owing to shooting behind the bird. The young shooter, as 1 observed before, must allow for the forward motion of the bird he aims at; and if at short distances, at larks and swamp blackbirds, he shoots ten or twelve inches ahead of the bird, he will be sure to hit it, provided the gun had the right elevation.

When the young shooter, after having missed two or three side shots, thinks it was owing tohis shooting behind his hirds, he must determine to hold ahead of the next that crosses. It is two to one that he will bring that one down, although he is but a beginner. The necessity of aiming ahead of crossing birds is often not thoroughly understood even by adult sportsmen whose practice has been large; and the distance at which it is proper to hold at a fast-flying bird crossing a long shot off is almost universally under-estimated. The gun at the shoulder must move with the bird until aim is taken the proper distance ahead of it. Then shoot instantly. The young shooter must practise all he can, neglecting no opportunity. When by proper instructions he has been taught what he is to do and how he is to do it, practice is the thing through which he will improve and perhaps become a first-rate shot. When he has been well entered at larks, swamp blackbirds, swallows and the like, he will be fit to go out with a companion, an old sportsman who knows how to manage dogs; if convenient, after game- birds.

Pinnated grouse, the young ones at the early part of the season, afford the very best practice for the beginners who have had some shootingat larks and blackbirds. If the commencement of the shooting season is changed by law from the fifteenth of August to the first of September, as I hope it will be, the young birds will still be sufficiently easy for the youthful sportsman. As it is now, they might be a little difficult on and after the first of September; for having been shot at almost incessantly for the last sixteen days in August, they have become rather wild, and the feeble ones have all been killed. I am satisfied that if the grouse season opened on the first of September, I could take a youth who had practised at larks and blackbirds, as above described, and had never seen a live grouse in his life, and so instruct him in the field by precept and example that his shooting should improve right along, so that late in October and November, he should often succeed in stopping grouse, when, according to some who call themselves sportsmen, they are so wild and difficult that they can't be killed with the gun at all. But as the young sportsmen of the East have no chance at the grouse of Illinois, Iowa, etc., and quail and snipe are. too difficult to afford fair practice for beginners, I should recommend the youthful gunners to try their hands at themigratory thrushes, called robins. These birds flock together in the fall before they go south, and fly up and down rows of trees in fields, or along fences, from tree to tree, in lanes, and about byroads. They will afford good practice. The beginner need not be deterred from shooting at them by the name " robin," because these birds are no more robins than woodcocks are. All three have red breasts, and so has the bullfinch.

The young shooter, as a matter of course, will not shoot at these handsome birds when they are about gentlemen's lawns, where they ornament the smooth-shorn turf and embellish the shrubbery. The time for action at them is when they flock preparatory to migration, when they will be found in such places as have been mentioned. The young sportsman may often be able to get shots at these birds sitting, but he should not take them. His main object is to learn to shoot well at birds on the wing, and to this end three so killed are of more account than three dozen shot sitting on tree-tops and on the boughs of scrub pines and cedars.

A boy who can bring down one-third of the larks and blackbirds he shoots at, and can stop a swallow once out of three or four times whenthey are flying low and darting a little, as they generally do before rain, is sufficiently advanced to go into the field after game. Once there, the same principles apply to him as ought to govern older marksmen, but do not always do so. During the first part of my residence in Illinois, although T was a good shot, as twenty brace of quail may serve to prove, I was nothing like as good as I have since become. Years of experience, shooting many months in each year, and nearly every day except Sundays, with much thought over the principles of shooting as an art, have enabled me to arrive at as much certainty as men attain to. It may seem like boasting, but nevertheless I declare my conviction that 1 can shoot game-birds on the wing, in the field, as well as any man who lives or ever did live. I have had a challenge out for three years, offering to shoot against any man in the world, Western field- shooting, and another offering to shoot against any man in the world at pigeons. The challenge for field-shooting has now been withdrawn, in consequence of the accident which befell me in 1872, when I was shot clean through the right thigh by my own gun when the muzzle touched me. It occurred in the way I shall now relate.

I was engaged in shooting pinnated grouse in December, in the neighborhood of Elkhart. On the ninth of that month, when starting at break of day, I drove to Mr. Gillott's pastures in my buggy, and got there before it was quite light. I opened the gate, went into the pasture, and, getting into the buggy again, prepared for shooting. The birds at that time were quite wild, and it was necessary to shoot them from the buggy. My gun lay upon my knees, both barrels cocked. As I was stooping over to draw the blanket upon my knees, the right fore-wheel of the buggy fell into a deep rut. The gun canted, and before I could catch it the butt hit the hind wheel, and the right barrel went off, making a hole through my thigh. The gun was loaded with five drams of powder and an ounce of No. 6 shot. It was a terrible wound, but happily most of the shot missed the thighbone. Some, however, hit it, but did not break it. They are in my thigh now. I drove home, was laid up four months, and am now well again. But the wound has had the following effect: I cannot walk as long as I used to do before I received it. It is also very painful at times, so much so that I almost fear it is going to breakout again. Now, under this altered state of things, it would hardly do for me to shoot against any man in the world, and see who could kill the most game in a week, say ; but I will even now shoot against any man in the world, for a reasonable number of hours on a reasonable number of days, and take shot about, as game offers, one man to follow the shot of the other. I shall now relate the methods I have finally adopted. To young sportsmen what I shall advance will certainly be instructive and useful, and I think many old ones may gather things from it which will be of service to them. One-half the shots made at birds in the field are at birds which fly across the shooter, presenting side shots, or go quartering off from him, so that their course forms an obtuse angle with the line of fire. Most of the misses which occur in shooting at such birds are owing to the failure of the shooter to hold forward enough so that the centre of the charge will be upon the bird when the shot reaches him. The centre of the flight of shot should reach the line of his flight just where he will be when the line of the shot intersects his line of flight, not where he was when the aim was made. The further the bird is from the shooter, the faster he is going, and the nearer his line of flight is at right angles with the line of the gun, the more the shooter must hold ahead of him to kill. I have had this very thoroughly impressed upon me since I have been a pigeon-shooter. When a man is in the field killing plenty of birds, and game is abundant, he does not pause to consider how it was he missed this bird or that. He pushes on to where his dogs have made another point. But when a man misses once or twice in ten birds from the traps, and there are five hundred or a thousand dollars depending upon his gun, ho is apt to cogitate over the reasons of these things.

I had already noticed that in field-shooting more of the birds got away crippled from side shots than from other kinds. The reason, I concluded, was simply this: the gun was not held quite forward enough, and, instead of being in the line of the centre of the charge, the bird was merely struck by one or two of the shot on the outer edge of the flight. If he was flying to the left, nothing but the outer shot on the left side would hit him ; and if to the right, nothing but the straggling outside shot on the right. I began to hold more forward at crossing birds, and then I found that instead of being hit and getting away crippled, the birds covered by the centre of the flying charge, or thereabout, were cut down dead.

In pigeon-shooting 1 soon made this principle a matter of nice calculation. Many may think that at only twenty-one yards from the trap there is no need for the practical application of this principle; but 1 know there is. At easy, slow flying birds, going right or left from the trap, I hold three or four inches ahead of the bird. It is well known by those who attend the great pigeon- shooting tournaments and matches that I generally kill all such birds, while some other men, who are very good shots, often miss them. The reason is plain to my mind: they shoot a little behind the bird. At a fast-flying crossing bird I hold from eight to ten inches ahead; at a quartering bird from three to four inches. At a bird which goes straight away close to the ground I hold right on, well covered, because he is rapidly advancing. At one going straight away and rising I shoot high, *because* he is rising, and if you hold right on to him you are apt to under-shoot; and though you may wound him, he will be likely to get out of bounds. At an incoming bird I shoot right at the head, and 1 rarely fail to kill. Incoming birds are often missed from under-shooting. The hardest of all birds are those which go straight away from the trap in the line of the shooter, at a very swift rate, and close to the ground. Such birds get hard hit, but they often get out of bounds. They present a very small mark; their wings are closed, perhaps, when the shot reaches where they are, the charge scatters, and their heads are covered by their bodies for the most part.

In field-shooting it is very necessary to apply the foregoing principles, because the bird shot at will often be forty yards off, and perhaps more. At a pinnated grouse going straight away the shooter should aim right on. When a side shot is presented, and the bird is going at a middling rate, thirty yards *off,* aim from ten to twelve inches ahead of it. Quartering shots must be judged of according to distance and rate of flight; taking my pigeon-shooting experience as a standard and guide, and remembering that late in the fall, when grouse rise far off and fly fast, the shooter must hold further ahead of crossing and quartering birds.

Some think that the barrels of a double-barrelled gun shoot a little in|that is, the right barrel shoots a little to the left, and the left barrel a little to the right. If some guns do this,they ought not to perform so. Good guns do not. I would not have a gun which shot in. It is wrong in principle.

At a quail flying fast across at twenty yards hold twelve inches ahead of the bird. Sometimes in quail-shooting a bevy put up by another sportsman near at hand will come by a shooter, crossing at immense speed thirty or forty yards off, perhaps more. In such a case hold three feet ahead of the bird you shoot at. I have often done so, and killed him. At ruffed grouse and woodcock in cover, and at pinnated grouse and quail in corn, snap-shots must be made. The sportsman must shoot at the glimpse of the bird, and, if he sees that it is crossing, a little in advance of it. A little will do in most cases, because the birds are hardly seen far off in thick cover or in corn. For snap-shooting of this sort a good-fitting gun is an absolute necessity, so that when it is tossed up it will come slap to the shoulder.

In duck-shooting, at the morning flights, when they are overhead and from thirty to forty yards in the air, hold from fifteen inches to two feet ahead of the bird you aim at, according to the rapidity at which it is moving. Great judgmentis to be exercised, and much practice is necessary to attain it. There is always a certain space of time between the aim and the arrival of the shot at the mark; and if the mark is moving across the muzzle of the gun, allowance must be made for it. Birds overhead are *always* crossing the muzzle of the gun, unless they see the shooter and tower up. After the taking of the aim, though ever so little after, the trigger has to be pulled, the hammer has to fall, the powder has to be ignited, and the shot to be propelled to the object shot at. Now, I often noticed that in shooting at the leading duck of a flock passing overhead which did not see me, and tower, I missed the one I shot at, and killed another one two feet behind the one which led the van and was aimed at. This made me resolve to hold more forward than I had been doing. Pintails and teal fly faster than mallards, and a little more allowance in taking aim will be good. I have seen a pintail killed which was three feet behind the duck shot at, and this more than once.

Wild geese and crane are slow flyers, and at these all that is necessary is to aim at the head, behind which there is the large body. But in shooting at wild geese and crane with large shot, andmaking a long shot, the shooter had better hold a little forward of the head of the bird. In windy weather the shot deflects somewhat from the straight course, and flies off a little to leeward. Allowance must be made for this, especially by those who use light charges of powder.

As to distance, there is this to be observed: although wild geese and ducks are almost always further off than they are supposed to be, they will be killed easily enough with a good gun and a proper charge, provided the gun is held right. I have often killed ducks and brant geese which were sixty yards off, and a few which were not less than a hundred. But there is no certainty of killing birds at more than forty yards, owing to the spread of the shot as it flies in diverging lines from the muzzle of the gun; and twice as many are killed at twenty-five yards and under as there are at over that distance. I have heard men boast of killing all the pinnated grouse they shot at within a hundred yards, and I immediately concluded that this might be true if they never shot grouse at any distance. It is like the story of the man who declared that his horse could run less than a mile a minute, whereupon an Irish jockey exclaimed: "That's a dld lie!"

I did once kill a pinnated grouse at ninety- five yards, but it was by a chance shot. I and Miles Johnson, of New Jersey, were shooting in McLean County with No. 7 shot. A pack of grouse got up together, of which he killed two and I killed two. One of the others circled round a long way off, and I slipped in another cartridge. The bird presented a long side shot, flying fast. 1 held as much as six feet ahead of him, and let fly. One of the shot happened to hit him in the head, and down he came with a heavy thud. Johnson stepped the ground from where 1 fired, and made it ninety-five yards to the dead grouse. It must have been as far off when the single shot killed it, for it fell perpendicularly, there being next to no wind. It was all a matter of chance. I had no expectation of killing the bird when I fired, and might shoot fifty times under the like circumstances without killing once.

I have recently visited the shot-tower of Tatham Brothers, and that of Thos. Otis Le Eoy & Co. The shot made at these towers is excellent. The latter is made according to the American standard adopted by the New York Sportsman's A sociation, which is as follows:

Scale. Number of Pellets
Diameter in inches. Number. to an ounce.
iVir TT 32
20 T! OQ
1OU ..... A CO
tfs BBB 44
stfff BB 49
tvO B 58
Tflr 1 69
Mb 2 82
ffc 3 98
fbao .4 121
Tft 5 149
-tfa 6 209
Tftr 7 278
Tott 8 375
rib- 9 .... /V/560
rSir 10 822
rfar 11 983
Tott 12 1,778

In reference to cartridge-cases, which I have had occasion to mention often, I shall here quote from the circular of the Union Metallic Cartridge Company, Bridgeport, Conn., for the information of sportsmen:

"Special attention is called to the Sturtevant Patent Movable Anvil. By the use of these anvils in metallic shells certainty of fire is secured, and the exploded caps are easily pushedoff without the necessity of any special instrument. The rod which is used for pressing down the wads in loading the shells will also answer for pushing off the exploded caps. These shells are intended to use the breech-loading shell-caps of our own make, or the English caps, such as used in Eley's paper shells, but in case of necessity the ordinary ' G. D.' caps may be used. These shells are made to fit the standard gauges used by the principal gun-makers of England, are sure to fit the chambers of the guns, and will stand reloading a great many times.

"The Sturtevant patent shells can be purchased of or ordered from any dealer in ammunition. Also metallic shells for shot-guns having the Berdan patent anvils, Nos. 1 and 2, and both metallic and paper shells with the Hobbs and Orcutt patent primers, which have the anvils secured in the caps."

CHAPTER XV.
SPORTING DOGS BREEDING AND BREAKING.

In my time I have bred and broken many dogs for the sports of the field, and always with a view to simple utility in the field. I think I have had some of the best dogs that a man ever shot over, and my system of breaking has always answered my purpose well; but I do not pretend to be a dog-breaker in regard to the particulars which many sportsmen hold to be necessary, but which I do not regard as essential in the light of my own experience. Therefore what I am about to say on this point is more for those who keep a dog or two of their own than for adepts in breaking dogs, or gentlemen who can afford to pay high prices in order to secure the results of high education in their pointers and setters. I propose to state on this subject what I know, and to mention some few facts in regard to dogs which I have bred, broken, and shot over which may serve to point the matter.

For the prairie country, where, as I believe, the best shooting within a thousand miles of the Atlantic seaboard is to be had, the setter is probably to be preferred. There are, however, several weighty matters which tell in favor of the pointer. The latter stands heat better than the setter, and there are many hot days in September, and even in October. Some think the pointer stands thirst better than the setter, but the truth is that both want water every hour and a half or two hours. The defects of the pointer for the prairie are his thin skin and tender feet. In the fall of the year the prairie-grass has a beard which cuts into skin or leather. Shoot in a pair of new boots, and the toes will be cut through in about ten days or a fortnight, or in less time, if you go into the dry grass much while the leather is still wet. Consequently, as the skin of the pointer is not protected by a thick coat of wiry hair, like that of the best and hardiest setters, it is cut on the legs, flanks, sides, and the inside of the thighs. The feet are also cut and lamed.

On the other hand, the long, thick coat of the setter gets full of cocide-burrs in those old fields in which game is often found, and they cause him a vast amount of trouble and annoyance. About one-fourth of the time in such fields thesetter is trying to free himself from the burrs, and at night, if they are not carefully picked out of his coat by his master, he gets no rest, and is nearly useless the next day. Sportsmen who shoot over setters should always, take care that they are freed from burrs in the evening. If they do not, their dogs will be miserable all night, and not fit for use in the morning, when the prime of the sport is to be had. I have had capital setters, and I must say that I have had and seen pointers in the field which were equally good, subject to the drawbacks I have mentioned above in regard to each.

Good dogs of both kinds have fine scenting powers, and the setters, so far as my experience goes, are as much under control as pointers when worked by men who know their business. Setters take to retrieving in water much better than, pointers, and on the whole, as I remarked before, the setter is the best dog for our part of the country. When the skin of the pointer *is* cut by the prairie-grass and rough weeds, and the tops of his toes are raw, he comes out in the morning so stiff and sore that he is hardly able to hobble along at first. The dog's ambition carries him on, however, and he gets more limberafter a while. But even then the flies settle on the sores and annoy him very much.

When Miles Johnson came out to Illinois to shoot with me, he had four as nice pointers as I ever saw, while I had one cross-bred dog between the pointer and the setter which he said did not look to be worth ten dollars. But the pointers, though used by turns, soon got sore, and, in order to make frequent changes, he had to take them out when they were hardly fit to go. My crossbred dog, on the contrary, was at work every day and never tired, so that Miles said many gentlemen in the East, if they saw his style of hunting, his staunchness, and the game and bottom he displayed, would give five hundred dollars for him. I have bred and used cross-bred dogs for years, and for the Western country, all sorts of work in the field or cover, long days and many days in succession, I hold them to be the best of dogs. I like to put a pointer-dog, well bred and good in the field, to a setter-bitch of the same excellent qualities, or a setter-dog to a pointer-bitch ; it makes no difference, that I could ever see, which side the pointer-blood was, though some have a theory that it does. Nor does it matter what the colors of the parents are. From a black setter-dog anda white pointer-bitch I bred a litter of liver- colored pups which became first-rate dogs.

Some of the cross-bred dogs take after the setter, and some after the pointer, in shape and coat, in the same litter. On the whole, I prefer those which follow the pointer. They have a short but thick coat and a tough skin, while the hair is not long enough to catch hold of the cockle-burrs. Both kinds are hearty, strong dogs, with good constitutions and capable of great endurance. As a rule, they are inclined to be headstrong and are difficult to break, but when they are broken and have learned their business they make first-rate dogs and hardly ever tire.

Those cross-bred dogs which take after the pointer look like pointers, and many men think they are pointers; but they have much better feet, and their legs and bodies are covered and well protected by thick but short hair. I have found them good, tough dogs, capable of standing more hard work than either pointers or setters, as a rule. Those which take after the setter have more power than setters, and great bone and substance. Their hair is not as long as the setter's, but it is thicker. Both kinds are as good for water and cold weather as need be. They have had plenty of both in my service, and I know the fact.

Another thing is that a timid dog is a rare exception among these cross-bred dogs. A timid dog gives immense trouble to breakers, and is, to my thinking, little better than a nuisance. A man must have great patience and forbearance to make much of timid dogs. If he corrects their faults, they are cowed at once, and slink behind his heels. The cross-bred dog, bold, high-headed, and eager, will run riot at first, but they can be educated and made to understand and perform their duties. They will stand punishment, and, in fact, cannot be broken without it; but when they are once well broken, they never forget what they have been taught to do or what to refrain from doing. As before remarked, I prefer those which follow the pointer in shape and coat, but I have had some which took after the setter, and were as nearly perfect as dogs could be. I think the best dog I ever had was one of these; at any rate she was esteemed by me as worth her weight in golfr.

Fanny was the produce of a pure-bred lemon and white setter-bitch, and a pure-bred livercolored pointer-dog. She took after her mother in shape and coat, but was larger and stronger, and was liver and white in color. She was of good size and strong. Her coat was thick and not as long as her mother's, and she had but a little feather on the legs. She had splendid scenting powers, was easily broken, was good for every sort of shooting, and the best retriever I ever saw. In retrieving pinnated grouse or quail, if she came upon the scent of other birds while bringing in the game, she would point and stand staunch with the dead one in her mouth, or even with a winged one that was fluttering. It is thought by some that a dog ought not to do this. I know that very few will do it with the winged bird, but I like it.

Fanny would work from daybreak until dark, and willingly. I shot over her seven seasons, and never knew her to " refuse" but twice, and on one of these occasions it was my fault, not hers. I killed thousands of birds over her, and broke many young dogs in her company. As a retriever of water-fowl I never saw her equal. She would cheerfully go in and bring ducks out of the water when ice froze in her hair as soon as she landed. It was in such weather that I fell into a great error, and caused her to refuse her work one time.

One very cold day I was shooting ducks on Salt Creek, and creeping up got a shot at a flock of mallards sitting on the water. It was a very large flock. One barrel was fired while they were on the water, the other as they rose. Eight were killed and five others winged. Fanny retrieved the dead ones, while the wounded swam to the other side of the creek and hid on the bank. She went to the other side, but the ice had now formed in her coat, and, being very cold, she sat down. I called her over to me and corrected her, after which she crossed and recrossed three times, and brought three more. She then wanted to give it up, and I had half a mind to let her do so; but there were two more ducks wounded, and if not brought they would die of slow starvation, so I required her to fetch them, which she did. It was a very hard task in such cold weather, and 1 was sorry to punish her; but it shows what this sort of dog can do when an emergency requires much strength and endurance. She was a very sagacious and affectionate bitch, and a great favorite in the house at home.

It is not good for a dog to be long in the waterin very cold weather. Fetching out one or two ducks does no harm, told good ones like it; but to be long in the water at such times is very trying. I never afterwards suffered Fanny to do more in that line than she could perform without injury.

Sometimes when going pinnated-grouse shooting, and passing along in my wagon early in the morning, I would have a chance to shoot one. On these occasions she would jump out, retrieve it, and jump back into the wagon with the bird in her mouth. If I drove for grouse in ploughed land or in grass-fields that had been mowed, with Fanny in the back of the wagon, she would, on seeing the birds, point from the wagon, and maintain her point all the while as I drove on to get within shot. One time, when going out for grouse to the Delavan Prairie, Fanny went into a corn-field at the edge of the timber, and I, paying no attention, drove on. Finding that she was not following, I pulled up, after having gone a considerable distance, and whistled for her. She stayed a long time, but came at last, bringing with her a wild turkey three parts grown. I had recently had her out when turkey-shooting, and she was the best dog I ever saw topoint a wild turkey. I have no doubt she stood at that turkey a long time, and only went in to catch it herself when called off. She could soon understand what I was after. If rabbit-shooting, she would stand and retrieve them, and, if not, she would not notice them.

Once, shooting pinnated grouse when they were wild, I found there was a flock on a fence two or three hundred yards off. I had a muzzle-loader, and hanging my shot-belt and powder-flask on the fence, I crawled up so as to be within shot when the grouse flew. I killed one, and winged another with the second barrel. In retrieving the wounded one Fanny winded a bevy of quail, and stood hard with the winged grouse fluttering in her mouth. The quail were twenty yards off from her in some corn, but nevertheless she stood hard and fast with the grouse fluttering in her mouth, while I went back two hundred yards for the powder and shot, loaded, and returned. I then took the grouse from her, whereupon she flushed the quail, and I killed a brace. This was one of the greatest things I have ever known a dog to do. The grouse was alive and fluttering; with a dead bird in her mouth the performance would not have been so very remarkable.

Fanny knew no fancy tricks, and would not fetch and carry out of the field. I have never taught my dogs out of the field. In the field no dog ever beat her. Her quick perception and sense were extraordinary. She seemed to understand what was wanted. If ducks in a pond were to be crawled up to, she would lie down as I started, and stay there until she heard the crack of the gun. If I laid anything down and told her to watch it, she always remained until I returned. If I had stayed away all day, or two days for that matter, she would not have left her post.

I have known dogs that could not be called off a point; but they were those which had been broken not to flush their game, leaving that to the shooter. An English gentleman came to Elk- hart from St. Louis, with whom I went shooting nearly every day during his visit. He had a pair of splendid pointers, as fine as I ever sawllarge, strong dogs with long heads. One of them was black, the other red. When the black dog would , get on a point in corn, he would not leave it until either his master or some other man flushed the birds. The consequence was that we often had to go in and find him, and I have frequently been half an hour in searching for him. That stylo of breaking may suit England well enough|no doubt it does; but in the prairie States it does not answer the purpose. The red dog was not so obstinately staunch. After standing his birds a good while he would flush them himself, and then come in sight of us. One day I wa3 prevented from shooting, and the gentleman came back at night without the black dog. He had lost him at dusk in a piece of prairie where the grass was tall. I saw the gentleman that night, and told him my opinion was that his pointer was in that piece of prairie, standing birds. At break of day the sportsman went out to the place, and there he found the dog, not standing up on his point|he was too tired for that|but sitting on his haunches. The grouse still lay to him, and the gentleman flushed it and shot it. This was his report to me. 1 saw him come in the previous night without the black dog, I saw him bring him home in the next forenoon, and I have no reason to doubt his veracity.

My famous Fanny died at work, as I may say. I was out with her one afternoon when there was good shooting, and finding that she did not want to continue at work, I put her into my wagon, and drove home. She did not appear tobe in pain; but as she had been in apparent good health in the morning, and had hunted with alacrity all the forenoon, I did not know what to make of it. She seemed to lose her strength, and yet I could not see any signs of her having been bitten by a poisonous snake or the like. In fact, I did not believe that she was seriously ill, and, having made up her bed nicely, I concluded she would be better in the morning. But that night she died, at nine o'clock. Fifteen minutes before her death she got up on her legs and looked at me very earnestly, as though she wanted to make me understand something. She then lay down again, and in fifteen minutes died easily. I had never left her after I brought her home, and her death was the cause of much grief in the family. It was almost as if we had lost one of the children. I do not know what her ailment was, but believe that she had an internal abscess, the bursting of which caused her death.

The best age to begin the breaking of a dog is about a year, in my judgment. At eight or nine months old it is well enough to take a puppy out to the field in a wagon, and let it work a little with an old dog. Care must be taken that young ones do not work much in the hot sun,for if they do there is an end to all reasonable hopes of their usefulness. They are spoiled for ever. What they are taught about a house or a yard is merely mechanical, in my opinion, and of very little service afterwards in the field. The field, where there are birds, is the place to break dogs, and puppies are too playful and too soft for the real breaking. At about a year old the dog is of an age to understand what is wanted of him in a short time, and also fit to endure the correction which will be required to make him avoid faults. It is better to begin with the young one in company with an old, staunch dog, as young dogs are imitative.

Some come to a point the first time they get on birds, but some do not, although their power of scenting may be very good. Some, when the old one points, run in, flush the birds, and then chase them. Many men think this grievous, but I invariably look upon it as a sign that the dog will make a good one, if properly handled and treated. Eagerness in the young dog indicates that the hunting instinct is strong, and then it only remains necessary to develop and govern it in the proper way. Some young dogs point larks and other little birds, and some men abhor this,but I like it. It indicates a good nose and the instinct to stand at point when the dog finds, and these are two of the main qualities upon which the future excellence of the youngster will depend. The best dogs I have ever had would point little birds around our house when puppies. The instinct of a young, unbroken dog does not instruct him as to what is game and what is not. They learn that in breaking and in after-use.

When a young dog runs in eagerly, there is no need to be harsh with him at first. It will be very easy to break him of that, and to make him comprehend that he is not to repeat it. My plan is to get young dogs eager after game, and then instruct them as to the method by which it is to be pursued and killed. Therefore I let them run in and chase a few times. The worst dogs to break are timid ones, which do not take much notice of birds, and are easily cowed. With these the utmost care and patience are required. With eager dogs after a little while I endeavor to make them understand that they are not to run in when the old dog points, but to back him. If they run in, then 1 whip them a little. If they persist in doing so after that correction, I take another method. Severe whipping does not answer the purpose for which it is intended. After being whipped once, the dog runs off when he finds he is likely to be whipped again. By the time he is caught and whipped again he has forgotten all about the original fault. Now, there is an effectual way to punish a fault at almost the moment of its commission, and thus to cure him of it without half the punishment of severe whipping.

I load one barrel with very small shot, No. 10. When the dog has had one or two warnings, and rushes in again as the old dog stands at point, I call " steady" in a loud, authoritative tone of voice. Then if he keeps on, flushes the birds, and chases them, I just give him some of the No. 10 on the quarters. lie will be at a good distance off, and the small shot will sting him sharply through his hair, but will not penetrate his tough skin. The dog knows in a moment what this is for. One lesson is generally enough, and the second is always effectual. A man might almost flay the hide off of some bold, headstrong dog with whips without breaking the dog to good purpose. My method obviates the necessity for a great deal of punishment with the whip, and is not really severe. A dog, however, should never be shot at with larger shot than No. 10, and never when he is not at the very least forty yards from the gun.

If a timid dog runs in and chases birds after they are flushed, let him do so for days without whipping him or shooting at him. The thing for him is encouragement to pursue game in any manner at first; and if he is whipped, he slinks behind his master's heels. Therefore his confidence must be increased and his instinct to hunt somewhat developed before he is taken in hand for his faults. On the other hand, the bold, headstrong dog, not easily cowed, may be quickly brought to terms. I do not teach my dogs to drop to shot, or down-charge, but I educate them to stand where they are when the gun is fired until told to go on. I can see no use in their dropping. The man remains standing, why not the dog 1 And besides, in hot weather, where the grass is long and the weeds tall and thick, it is injurious to the dog to lie down, because he gets less air than he does on his legs. I think dropping to shot and down-charging better dispensed with in these days of breech-loaders; still, I do not mean to set up as an authority on dog-breakingII simply give the results of my own experience and observations.

One of the best dogs I ever owned was a red setter, named Jack, a large, strong, upheaded dog. I bred him myself, and sold him when a pup to a butcher. With plenty to eat and nothing to do he grew up big, and was always fat. The butcher had him until he was two years old, and thought a good deal of him, though he never used him in the field or anywhere else, except as a watch-dog and to follow his meat-wagon. The butcher died when Jack was two years old, and I bought him of the widow. -He was entirely unbroken when I took him out with a steady old dog. The latter got a point, and thereupon Jack ran in, flushed the birds, and chased them. After he had gone forty or fifty yards I hallooed at him, but he did not notice it. I knew what he would do, as his parents were both high-headed, bold-ranging dogs, and he was given to riotous frolicking and full of pluck. I had loaded both barrels of my gun expressly for his benefit, and now shot at him. The distance was rather long, but he was well stung. Nevertheless, he did not mind it, and kept on. Thereupon I let him have the other barrel, upon which he came back. At the next point at pinnated grouse in prairie-grass Jack ran in again. I hallooed, but he kept on, and again I shot at him; then he came back. Once again he started to run in, but upon my hallooing " Steady! " ho halted, and backed the point of the old dog. This was the first point he ever made in his life, and he hardly knew whether it was right or not. I went up and petted him, upon which he give indications that he understood what he was wanted to do. From that out he backed the old dog well. He was a little eager afterwards, but upon the whole 1 consider him to have been the easiest-broken dog that I ever handled.

He took to retrieving, and was a rare good one at it; in duck-shooting, one of the best I ever had. In retrieving ducks he went at a gallop, swam as fast as he could, and brought in the dead at his best pace. There was no loafing about or slow walking with the duck in his mouth in his way of doing the work. A slow retriever for ducks is not good. -While he is fooling about a flock or two of ducks, seeing him, sheer off, and the shooter loses chances which he might improve. When retrieving grouse or quail, Jack would point live birds with a dead one in his mouth. He was very eager to have the gun kill, and at length appeared to think that I must have killed something every time I fired a shot. This uncommon eagerness and resolution of his gave rise to a ludicrous incident.

I was going with another man to shoot grouse late in the fall, and we had Jack and two other dogs in the wagon. A flock of brant were upon the prairie, and though they rose far off, we fired, but did not kill. Jack jumped out, and seemed to think it impossible that there was nothing killed or wounded. About that part of the prairie there were some poor, lean sheep suffering from foot-rot. Upon one of the smallest of these little sheep Jack seized, and began hauling it towards the wagon. I thought my partner would almost die of laughing. I made Jack leave the sheep and come into the wagon again.

I afterwards sold this dog to Benjamin McQueston, a gentleman who then lived at Springfield, Illinois, but who now lives somewhere in Kansas, where he still has Jack. I ought not to have parted with the dog, but Mr. McQueston was very anxious to get him, and paid a good price, for our part of the country. The way of it was this: Four of us, including the gentleman mentioned, had been out shooting, and were returning along the road with a wagon and team. Jack had performed a good day's work, but was still full of spirit and vigor, anxious to hunt. As we drove along, he jumped on a rail-fence to leap down into the field on the other side, and right there he winded a bevy of quail. With his fore-feet on the top rail and his hind ones on the second Jack came to a dead point, and made as pretty a one as was possible in the position. Thereupon Mr. McQueston resolved to have him, if 1 could be prevailed upon to sell. There is not a dog in the country 1 would prefer to Jack to breed from.

The best dog I have now is Dick, eight years old and cross-bred, being the produce of a setter-bitch and a pointer-dog. His color is red, and he takes after the setter, but has thicker and shorter hair. He is a capital worker, and an excellent dog for finding game. I did not breed him myself, but I broke him, he being two years old when I got him. He had been used in the field a little, but was worse than if he had never been out at all. I found him a high-headed, eager, headstrong dog, such as I always think will make a good one. I brought him into theproper way of working by stinging him with shot once or twice when ho was going on wrong. He is now an excellent dog. I do not teach my dogs to retrieve, but let them take it up of their own accord from seeing my old dogs do it. About half learn to retrieve in that way. They could all bo taught to do so easily enough.

The most thorough dog-breaker 1 know is Miles Johnson, of Yardville, New Jersey. lie has a capital place to keep dogs, and is a perfect master of the art of breaking them, retrieving, and everything else which may be thought desirable. I recently saw at his place a liver and white setter which he has broken to do almost anything. This is the most perfectly-educated sporting dog I ever saw; and if gentlemen want their dogs educated in this way, Johnson is the man to do it.

My method is very serviceable, and includes all that 1 deem essential, but many would want more to be done with them. There is one thing sportsmen should always persevere in, and that is, making the dog perform what he undertakes to make him do. I never let a dog evade doing what I have set out to make him do. Your dogs must be made to understand clearly that you are the master, and that your will ia to rule their in-

clinations. When Fanny was young and a pretty good dog, retrieving grouse very nicely, on one hot morning she refused to find and bring in a grouse I had shot. She ran for the corn, whereupon I fired over her and stung her with two or three straggling shot. She kept on, however, and bolted for home, some four miles distant. I knew that would never do, and, jumping into my buggy, I drove off and got there before she did. When she came jogging on, she seemed astounded at seeing me there. I gave her a few cuts with the whip, and took her back to the place where she had misbehaved, upon which she found tho dead bird, and brought it in. If I had passed that over, she would have gone off again on some day when she was more inclined for rest than work. When a dog runs off instead of doing what -he is required to do, bring him back to the same place, no matter at what trouble, and compel him to perform it. If young sportsmen neglect this, and go on their way rather than lose a little time, their dogs will find it out, and do pretty much as they like. It is this which causes many dogs which have really been well broken to turn out to be rascals in their owners' hands.

Cross-bred dogs are seldom good beyond thefirst cross, though some bred from mine and the Scotch sheep-dog have turned out very well. But the sheep-dog has a fine nose and amazing sagacity, with a grand capacity to receive education and retain its fruits.

The first dogs I shot over were cocking-spaniels, and I do not believe they had any breaking at all. I recently visited the neighborhood in which 1 learned to shoot on the wing, and the fine farm of Mr. Jeremiah Rundell, at Stoekport, on the Hudson Eiver, over which I used to shoot. With him and his family I ate some splendid apples, the produce of an orchard whose trees I helped to plant eighteen years ago.

SECTION 15

CHAPTER XVI.
   PIGEON-SHOOTING.
   I Began to shoot pigeons in 1868, when I had been a field-shot for more than eighteen years. 1 had often been invited to go and witness contests of the kind, but cared nothing for them, and up to 1868 had never seen a pigeon-trap. The first public pigeon-shooting into which I entered was a series of sweepstakes at St. Louis. I had some success; so much, in fact, that R. M. Patchen, who was with me, forthwith made a match, in which I was to shoot against Gough Stanton of Detroit for $200 a side. Expenses were to be paid to whomever travelled to the other, and he came to Elkhart. The match was fifty birds each, He brought with him a plunge trap, the first I had ever seen of that character. However, I consented to the use of it, and won by killing forty-six to his forty. I was then just about as good a shot at pigeons as I am now, except that I was anxious about the money, and sometimes missed owing to that.
   The Champion MedaL
   I next shot against Abraham Kleinman. John Thomson, a stockman of Elkhart, made the match on my part. It was for $200 a side, fifty birds each from a spring-trap. There was a dispute about the quantity of shot to be used, he contending that it was to be limited to an ounce. We made a sort of compromise, by which I was to pull my

own trap, while he was allowed a man to pull for him. The match was trap and handle for each other. He had an old trapper named Farnsworth to do this on his part, while my man, as afterwards appeared, did not know an old bird from a young one. Before we began I offered to bet that I killed forty-six out of fifty. This wager was eagerly accepted by Farnsworth, who wanted to bet a larger sum on the point. Kleinman killed forty-nine and I killed forty-six. I told Kleinman that I could and would beat him before long, and went home to practise in the field. 1 challenged him for the championship of Illinois, and we shot for $200 a side, at fifty single birds and twenty-five pairs of double birds eachlthe single birds ground-trap, the doubles plunge-traps. Of the single birds 1 killed forty-three to Klein- man's forty-two. At the doubles we killed fortythree each. It was at Chicago in 18G8. Soon after I shot with another man two or three times, and won; but I shall not mention his name in this book, for sufficient reasons:

The next match I took up with Abraham Kleinman was rather singular in character. It was at single and double birds. I was to shoot from a b.uggy at twenty-one yards, the horse to be on a trot or run when the trap was pulled. Kleinman shot from the ground at twenty- five yards. I won it. I afterwards shot two other matches on these conditions, one with King at Springfield, and one with Henry Conderinan at Decatur. Of these I lost one, and won the other. My shooting from a buggy at plover, grouse, and geese had made me very quick and effective.

In the spring of 1869 E. M. Patchen made a match, in which I was backed to kill five hundred pigeons in six hundred and forty-five minutes, with one gun, at Chicago. 1 was to load my own gun, and the stakes were $1,000 a side. There were heavy outside bets that I could not do it. I won the match, however, in eight hours forty-eight minutes, and thus had one hour fifty-seven minutes to spare. In the third hundred pigeons1 killed seventy-five in consecutive shots. In the last one hundred and five birds I scored one hundred; and in the seventh hour killed ninety- five. I shot with a muzzle-loader. It was twenty- one yards rise and fifty bounds. Before this match came off I had, in practice, killed five hundred birds in five hours and seven minutes; but then I used two guns, and had a man to clean them, though I loaded them myself. I missed thirty-four out of the whole number shot at.

I was next matched to kill a hundred consecutive birds at Chicago in July, 1869; $1,000 to $100 that I could not do it, and three matches to be shot if I failed in the first and second. In the first I had killed thirty when the lock of my gun broke, and being obliged to borrow one which was a poor article, I lost. On the 21st of the month I tried it again, and won. At Detroit in the same season I undertook to kill forty birds in forty minutes, to load my own gun, and gather my own birds. I killed fifty- three in twenty minutes forty seconds, and won. In the fall of 1869 I shot a match for $1,000 a side against King at Chicago. It was fifty single birds and fifty pairs of double birds, making one hundred and fifty each, plunge-traps, twenty-one yards rise. I killed all my single birds. Mr. King killed forty-one of his. I killed eighty-five of my double birds, Mr. King seventy- five of his.

I shot and won a great many matches which I need not mention here. In 1870, Mr. Nathan Doxie challenged any man in Illinois to go to his place and shoot against him for $100 at twenty-five birds. 1 went there and killed twenty-two to his twenty-one.

At the Chicago tournament I killed ten straight at twenty-one yards, as did several others. Under the conditions we went back to twenty-six yards to shoot the ties off at five birds each. Mr. G. K. Fayette, of Toledo, Ohio, and I tied four times more at this distance, killing all our birds. I then killed five more, making twenty-five consecutive birds at twenty-six yards. Mr. Fayette killed four of his last five, but missed the fifth, so I won. Later on I shot against Mr. J. J. Kleinman, of Chicago, at five traps, fifty birds, mine at twenty-eight yards rise, his at twenty-five. I won, and in the course of the match killed thirty-three consecutive birds.

At Detroit, in the fall of 1870, I shot my first match with Ira Paine, of New York, for $500 a side. It was a hundred birds each, twenty-one yards rise, eighty bounds, half from ground-traps, half from plunge-traps. We shot from the ground-traps first. When we had each shot at seventy birds, I was seven ahead, and night was coming on, so Paine gave it up. At that time he held the champion badge, and exhibited it to us at Detroit, whereupon Doxie told him to make much of it, for that I would go to New York to shoot for it and bring it away. I soon after challenged for it, and on the twenty-fifth of January, 1871, we shot for it at the house and grounds formerly kept by Hiram Woodruff, on Long Island. Paine killed eighty-eight birds to my eighty-five, and retained the badge. I used a breech-loader in that match. We then agreed to shoot at one hundred birds each, ground-traps, for six consecutive days, the stake each day $500, and either party refusing to go on to the end of the sixth match to forfeit $100. On the first day I killed eighty to Paine's sixty-two, and then he paid forfeit rather than go on; but he backed John Taylor against me at fifteen single birds and ten pairs of double birds, twenty-one yards rise, one ounce of shot. I killed fourteen of the single birds; Mr. Taylor killed nine. I shot at eight pairs of double birds, and killed twelve; he at nine pairs, and killed ten, and then gave up.

On that same visit to New York I was backed to kill forty-five out of fifty, with leave to place the trap as I pleased. The arrangement of the trap was objected to by Mr. Robinson's umpire, because it was so contrived that it would open towards the shooter first. The referee decided that the trap could not be so placed, and I turned the trap and missed six out of ten, and lost. Thereupon Mr. De Forrest offered to bet $250 that I could not kill forty-five out of fifty, and fix the trap my own way. It was not a bad bet on his part, for the difference in the mode of fixing the ground-trap is not a great advantage to the shooter, and Mr. Robinson had brought clipping-birds for me to shoot at. However, I scored forty-six, and won.

At Lincoln, Illinois, I shot against Abraham Klcinman at one hundred birds each, one ounce of shot, and each of us killed eighty-eight. We had not birds there to shoot the tie off, so we adjourned to meet at Chicago, where he killed ninety-one and I killed ninety, losing by one bird. With Ira Paine I have shot ten matches and won eight.

One other match I shall mention here because of its novelty. At Chicago I shot against four of the best marksmen in Illinois. The gentlemen opposed to me were Abraham Kleinman, Abner Price, D. T. Elston, and Benjamin Burton. They were selected to shoot in company at fifty birds each, all they scored to form an aggregate, while I was to shoot at two hundred birds. I won the match by killing one hundred and seventy-eight birds, while the four who contested it with me shot exceedingly well themselves by scoring one hundred and seventy-six.

It is proper that I should give here a few hints to the members of new shooting-clubs, and to some of those who belong to older institutions, in order that they may not be placed under disadvantages when they enter upon contests of a public nature. Since I began to shoot pigeons I have travelled a great deal, shot a great deal, and observed the performances of all sorts of men. The one great thing for new clubs to observe is this: that in their shooting at home, whether for practice or in contests with each other, they should follow the rules

16

SECTION 16

of pigeon-shooting, and not go on under loose, lax methods. It is essential that the rule as to holding the gun should be habitually complied with|that is, the butt must be kept below the elbow of the shooter until the bird is on the wing. It is just as easy to conform to this rule as not, provided it is done habitually and constantly, and it will save a great deal of trouble when public matches or sweepstakes are engaged in. If it is not regarded at home in their own clubs, the shooters will be certain to have birds decided lost which they have killed, when shooting elsewhere, by reason of breach of this rule. When several men are shooting- at home, that is the place to learn to shoot according to the rules. If they are disregarded, the club and its chosen marksmen will pay the penalty of their neglect another day, wher. there will be a smart to it.

Therefore I say it is better for members of these clubs to pay for a few birds at home, by enforcement of the rules, than to be beaten elsewhere through having dead birds challenged for improper holding of the gun. I have acted as referee many times, and have seen numbers of birds killed in such a manner that if anappeal had been made, I should have been compelled to decide against the shooters for having brought up the gun to the shoulder too soon. It is better to get used to holding the gun well down. When the habit is formed, a man can shoot as well that way as the other, and then he will not be bothered and confused by being challenged under the rule in a strange place. Conform to the rules at home, and it will be easy to observe them abroad. Shooters need not suppose that they will not be enforced in other places because they have been accustomed to disregard them at home.

When I first commenced pigeon-shooting, I lost a match in consequence of having two birds decided against me for holding the gun above the elbow before the pigeons flew. Since then I have always been careful to hold the gun well down, in practice as well as in matches and sweepstakes. Another thing to be noted is this: in club-shooting, where eight or ten of the members contend, the birds should be assorted| the old ones put into one basket and the young ones into another; and then they should be apportioned to the shooters equally. When the old ones and the young are all mixed up, thereis an element of chance brought in. One man may happen to get nearly all fast, driving birds, and another all slow, easy ones. Now, that is not the way to find out the best shooters. The more the element of chance is admitted, the less likely skill with the gun is to win. A fast, driving bird is killed, but gets out of bounds. A slow one is not hit half as well, but drops inside, and is scored. But the man who lost his bird really made the best shot.

If I had to make rules to govern pigeon- shooting, I should establish a new principle by sweeping away an old but mischievous rule. I would adopt the Prairie Club rules of twenty-one yards rise for single birds, and eighteen for double birds; but I would do away the boundary limit altogether. If the shooter recovered his bird within three minutes, he should count it, subject, of course, to the rules as to mode of recovery. When a man makes a splendid shot at a fast, driving bird, and it falls dead just out of bounds, it is decided against him by the arbitrary nature of the rule merely, and not by the principles of reason and sense. I have no individual interest to promote by suggesting this change. I find myself excluded from about nine out of every tenpublic contests by reason of my alleged superiority, and really see but little or nothing left for me to do save defend the championship.

Therefore what I advance is prompted solely by considerations for the sport, for the benefit of the clubs, and for the advancement and reward of real skill. There is no other way of absolutely determining which man is the best shot on the day of the contest. I have often killed birds which fell just out of bounds, riddled through and through with shot, and 1 have seen other men do the same. Birds hit like this, with seven or eight shot in each, were lost by a few feet, sometimes by a few inches, and I contend that this tape-line rule is against sense, and productive of mischief. I have seen hundreds of birds lost under the operation of it which were as well hit as any birds could be, so far as the skill of the marksman can go. On the other hand, I have seen easy, slow-going birds, just hit with one or two pellets in the wing, recovered amongst much clapping of hands and shouting by those who thought they were applauding marksmanship.

Recently the Buffalo gentlemen, in shooting for the Dean Richmond Cup, had their chance jeoparded at one time through three of Mr. Newell'sbirds, fast, driving ones, falling out of bounds, though hit clean and well. And irr my opinion he made as good shots at them as at any that ho scored, if not better. Every pigeon-shooter of large experience knows that matches are sometimes lost by the man who shoots best, because of his hard luck in having birds fall dead just out of bounds. Now, there ought to be as little chance for luck in contests of this nature as may be possible to contrive.

I have many times killed every bird I shot at, but some fell out of bounds. Now, if shooting is the thing to be tested, I had as much right to these, which were killed by the gun, as to those which fell inside. At Omaha, last June, I shot at fifty birds, twenty singles and fifteen pairs of doubles. I killed all the single birds, but lost one by reason of its falling a little out of bounds. I scored all the double birds, thus making forty-nine out of fifty, and if it had not been for the senseless, arbitrary rule in question, 1 should have scored all the fifty.

The fair way to shoot pigeons, whether in clubs, matches, or sweepstakes, is from H and T traps, no matter whether ground, plunge, or spring traps. In matches, the birds being in the traps, and the shooter ready, the referee tosses up a coin. If it comes head, the shooter takes the H trap and his opponent the other. If it comes tail, the effect is the reverse. In club-shooting and in sweepstakes as many wads are numbered as there are shooters. The referee places these in his pocket, and after shaking them up pulls one out. The man whose number on the list corresponds to the number on the wad takes the bird in the trap. That wad is then transferred to the other pocket. After the shot another wad is drawn, and so on until all have shot, when the wads will all be in one pocket, and the same thing is to be done until the shooting is at an end. By this means all trickery and favoritism in selecting birds for certain of the shooters is made impossible. I shall now append the scores of the nine championship matches by which the possession of the badge has been determined. The rules under which it was held and shot for will be given hereafter. It was required to be held for two years against all comers before it became the property of the holder. I have held it over three years now, having put it up again last spring, when John J. Kleinman shot against me for it at Joliet. Illinois.

It was first shot for at Mark Rock, Rhode Island, at thirty-five birds each; entries: Miles L. Johnson of New Jersey, Edward Tinker of Rhode Island, Perry Aldridge of Rhode Island, Ira A. Paine of New York, J. R. Brown of Buffalo, and John Taylor of New Jersey. It came off April 7, 1870, and was won by Johnson, the score being as follows:

Johnson|1101111111011111111011111 111111111|32.
Taylor| 0 110011111110111111101111111 111111111|30.
Tinker| 11111011101111111011010111 11111111 1|30.
Paine|11111001101101111011011111
0 1 i 11 11 1|28.
Bkown| 1 11011111111011111100011001111011 1|27.
Aldridge|11111011101010011111111111 110111011 0|27.

Paine challenged Johnson, the holder of the badge, and they shot at one hundred birds at Fleetwood Park, New York, September 28, 1870. Paine won as follows:

Paine|1 1111111101111110110001111 111111110111110111111111110111111 0111111111011111011111011111111101
 1 010111|85.

Johnson|110100111111100100001111 11111101000110110111111111111110 00011111111111110111111011111111 111110110|77.

120 FIELD, COVER, AND TRAP SHOOTING

Tinker challenged Paine, and they shot at Fleet- wood Park, October 29, 1870. Paine won as follows :
Paine|1111111011111111111111100111 11111111111111111111111111100111110 110110111111101101111011101110111 1111011|86.
Tinker|1 10111110111111000110111111010101011011111111101111111111 111110011011101111111111011111111
1101111 0|81.
A. H. Bogardus of Illinois challenged Paine, and they shot at Hiram Woodruff's old place on Long Island, January 25, 1871, when Paine won as follows :
Paine|11111111101111101111111111 11111111111111111111111011001111111 11100110101111111111111011011101 1111111|88.
Bogardus| 111111110011111111111101 111010110111101011011111111111 1110110111111011111111011101111 1111101111|85.
Bogardus challenged Paine, and they shot at Fleetwood Park, May 23, 1871, when Bogardus won as follows (besides, he killed seven which fell out of bounds) :
Bogardus|11111111011111111011111111 11111111111101111110111101111011111 1011111101100111111111111110101110111111 1|87.
Pahhs|11101111111111111111111110101101111111111110100110111011011 01011111111111101111111111111011 111111 1|86.
Paine challenged Bogardus, and they shot at Dexter Park, Chicago, July 29, 1871. Bogardus won as follows:
Bogardus|11111111101111111101111 1111111111111111111011111111111011 J 111011011111111110111111111111 11101110 1|91.
Paute| 11111111101111111111111011 111111111110111010110110111111111 11111111111100111111111111111111C1 1110111|89.
Abraham Kleinman of Illinois challenged Bogardus, and they shot at Dexter Park, Chicago, April 6, 1872, when Bogardus won as follows:
BOGAKDUS|1 11 1101111 11111101111111 1111011111111111111011111111111011 111111111111011111111111111111111
11111110 1|93.
Kleinman| 1111111111101111111110 11111111111111111111111111101111111 11110111101111101110111111110 111011011 0|89.
[These are the official aggregates of the match, but not of the details, which could not be obtained.]
Abraham Kleinman challenged Bogardus again, and they shot at Dexter Park, Chicago, in September, 1872, when Bogardus won as follows:
Bogardus|1 101101111111110111101011111011011111111011010111111001 111111111111111111111111010111 11101111 1|85.
Klblnmah|1 11111110110111011110111110011111111011011111111111111 110111100111110111111111111110 111101011 0|84.
Tinker of Rhode Island challenged Bogardus, and they shot May 15, 1873, at Dexter Park, Chicago, where Bogardus won as follows:
BOGARDUS|1 11011101111011111111111 11111111111111111111111111101111101 111110010111110111111011110111 01111111 0|87.

| 1 111101111111111111111111111 0111111001111111101011111111111011 11100111111 1111011 1|85.

Bogardus having now held the badge over two years, it became his property. He put it up again under the rules which are inserted hereafter. John J. Kleimnan, of Chicago, entered to contend for it, and Bogardus and he shot at Joliet on the twentieth of March, when Bogardus won. It remains with Bogardus, and will be open to challenge up to twentieth of March, 1876.

The scores of a few of my best matches, other than for the championship, are given below, and also some of my time matches :

Bogardus against King at Chicago, Dexter Park, 1809, single birds, fifty each, and fifty pairs of double birds each, $1,000 a side, twenty-one yards rise. This was the first match in which Bogardus shot with a breech-loader. It was one of the best scores he ever made, all at 21 yards.

SINGLE BIRDS.

BOGARDtTS|1 111111111111111111111111111 1111111111111111111111111 1|50 OUt Of 50.

King|1 11111110010111110111110010l 11111110101111111111|41 out of 50.

DOUBLE BIRDS.

BOGABDUS|11 11 11 11 11 10 11 11 11 10 11 10 11 11 10 11 11 11 11 11 10 11 11 11 01 10 11 11 01 11 11 11 11 11 11 11

111110 11 10 10 10 10 10 11 10 11 11 11|85.

King|10 111111 10 11 111110 11 00 10 11 10 11 10 11 1111 10 1110 01 10 11 1111 11 11 10 11 11 11 00 00 11 11 10 10 11 11 11 10 10 00 10 1111 10 11|75.

The following is the score of the match against time, shot at Dexter Park, Chicago, May 15, 1869, in which I undertook to kill five hundred pigeons in ten hours and forty-five minutes with one gun, and load my own gun. I did it in eight hours and forty-eight minutes, with !(of shot, ground trap.

First Hundred| 1 1111101000111101111 1 111101011011010011111001110111111 0111100001010111010011011110111111 11101111101111010011110111111101111 1111101C 1|136 shot at; 36 missed.

Second Hundred|1 01110101101101011111 11111010110111111111111111011001011 101111011011101111011011111111110 111110100101011010001101101011110 11111111| 0 0–138 phot at; 38 missed.

Third Hundreiv|0 11010101011010111010 1001111110011111111111111111111111 111111111111111111111111111111111 111111111111111111111011111 1|114 shot at; 14 missed.

Fourth Hundred|1 111111110111101111 1 1101111111111101110101111111110111 100110111111111111111111111111111 11111011111111110111111111 | 112 shot at; 12 missed.

Fifth Htodked|11101111111111111110 111111111111111111111111111111111 1111111111101111111111111111111 1 1111110111111011 1|105 shot at ; 5 missed. Time|8h. 48m.

Score of the match to kill one hundred birds in one hundred successive shots, and load as I pleased, shot at Dexter Park, Chicago, July 21, 1869:

111111111111111111111111111111111 1111111111111111111111111111111111
11111111111111111111111111111111111

Below will be found the scores of a few exhibition matches shot by me within a year.

At Jerseyville, Illinois, 1873, to kill fifty birds in eight minutes:

1111111111111111111101111111111111 1111111111111111111111 1|53 out of 54. Time of shooting|4m. 45s.

Captain A. H. Bogardus, match at Paris, Ky., April 14, 1874, to kill fifty pigeons in eight minutes :

11 11 11 11 11 11 111110 10 10 1111111110 1111 1111 11 11 11 11 00 11 11 11 00 11 11 11 10 10 |Killed, 58; misses, 10 ; number shot at, 68 ; time of shooting, 7m.

Match at Stamford, Conn., 1874, to kill thirty-eight out of fifty birds, two traps forty yards apart, to be pulled at the same time, and the shooter to stand between the traps. Ira Paine trapped the birds:

10 11 10 11 10 11 1111 11 1111111111111111111110 11|Killed 38 out of 42.

Match at Omaha, purse of $150, same conditions as at Stamford; shot June 19, 1874:

11 11 11 11 10 1111 1110 11111111 1111 11 11 10 1110 11 10|Killed 39 out of 44.

Score made by me on the same day in a sv/eep-stakes:

Sraaus Birds|111111111111011111111|19 killed, 1 missed.

Double Birds|11 1111 1111 1111111111111111111 11|30 killed.

Aggregate|49 out of CO.

Match at Washington, D. C., July 20, 1874, on the grounds of the Shooting Club. Colonel Alexander pulled the traps, which were forty yards apart:

1111 111111111111 11 1111 10 11 11 11|29 out of 80.

In this match at Washington I shot with the Orange powder of Laflin & Rand, New York, No. 7 Lightning, and found it strong and clean, and better than any I ever used before. I shot at one bird full seventy-five yards off, let go by an outsider, and killed it dead. It is coarsegrained, burns even, does not recoil much, and shoots strong.

CHALLENGES FOR FIELD AND TRAP SHOOTING.

The following challenges, made by me, and published in the sporting papers, were not accepted :

(From the Chicago Tribune.)

A CHALLENGE.

I hereby challenge any man in America to shoot a pigeon match, fifty single and fifty double rises, for from $500 to $5,000 a side, according to the rules of the New York Sportsmen's Association; 1 to use my breech-loading shot-gun, and my opponent to use any breech-loading gun of any manufacture ho may choose. The match to be shot in Chicago. Man and money ready at my place of business, No. 72 Madison Street, Chicago. A. H. Bogardus.

Chicago, Sept. 10, 1869.

CHALLENGE FOR FIELD SHOOTING.

To The Editor Of The Chicago Tribune :

I hereby challenge any man in America to shoot prairie-chickens against me, in the field, during the month of November, to shoot for one or two weeks, . on the same ground, for a stake of from $]00 to $500 a side. The man who kills the most during the time specified to take all the game and the stakes.

A. H. Bogardus. Chicago, Sept. 22, 1869.

Challenges For Field And Pigeon Shooting.

Editors Turf, Field, And Farm :

I notice in your issue of the 3d inst. an acceptance of my challenge, which was issued last October. This is the first I have ever seen of it, and that time has gone by; and if Mr. Murphy wished to shoot with me,- he couldhave easily dropped me a few lines, and I would have hunted with him. But all I can say now is (to Mr. Murphy or any other man living), that I will make a match to shoot in the field for two or four weeks next November; the kind of game to be prairie-chickens, the hunting to take place on strange ground to both parties, and the stakes from $500 to §2,000 a side, to hunt through the day-time and sleep at night, and not to take any advantage of the game; and also, if the party who accepts this challenge choose, that every bird has got to be killed on the wing; and if either party kill birds sitting, to count three against him.

Now, if Mr. Murphy and his friends think that I am playing a game at bluff, let them send a forfeit to the *Turf, Field, and Farm,* and I will cover it. The match to come off in November next in Illinois, Iowa, Minnesota, or Kansas, or any other place where we can find plenty of chickens. The man who wins to take the proceeds of all chickens shot by both parties. Yours very truly,

A. H. Bogardus. N.B.|I hereby challenge any man in the worldto shoot a match at pigeons, one hundred single and fifty double rises, for a stake of $1,000 to $2,000 a side; the birds to be put into one basket or box, and trap and handle out of same lot of birds, or from H and T traps, one or one and a half ounce shot. Will give or take expenses. A. H. B.

Elkhabt, Ill., May 8, 1872.

Rules governing the Badge held by the Champion Pigeon-Shooter of America.

We, the undersigned, contestants for the badge of the championship of America, given by the Rhode Island Sportsman's Club, do hereby pledge ourselves and agree to the following rules and regulations, whenever and wherever said badge is contested for:

1. The winner of the badge shall give a satisfactory guarantee to the officers of the Rhode Island Sportsman's Club for the safety thereof, in the shape of a responsible surety.

2. The winner shall pledge himself to shoot any challenger for a sum not less than $500 a side, within four months of the date of said challenge, under penalty of forfeiting the badge.

3. Any party challenging the holder of this badge shall make a deposit of $250 as a forfeit for a match of $500 a side, in the hands of the editor of the *Spirit of the Times,* to be covered by the challenged party with an equal amount. The balance of the money, $250 a side, shall be deposited in the hands of the said editor of the *Spirit of the Times,* or some party appointed by him, three days before the match is shot;

said match then becoming play or pay. In case of the holder not complying with the foregoing conditions, he shall forfeit the badge to the party challenging.

4. Every contestant for this match shall pledge himself to contend for the same under the rules of the Rhode Island Sportsman's Club governing pigeon-shooting.

5. All matches for this badge shall be at one hundred single birds each, H and T ground-traps.

6. In all matches in which this badge is contested for, the referee shall be an officer in the Rhode Island Sportsman's Club, or a party approved by them.

7. The holder of the badge shall name the place where the same shall be contested for, which shall be also satisfactory to the referee.

8. Each contestant in any match for this badge shall provide not less than one hundred and ten birds for the match, and the birds shall be taken out of one contestant's basket or box till the same is exhausted, and then the other contestant's basket or box shall be used out of till that is exhausted, and so on alternately through the match.

9. Having tossed for first shot and trap, the second party shooting shall take the bird in the remaining trap, and so on through the match.

10. The party holding this badge for two years against all contestants, it shall become his personal property.

Mules of the Rhode Island Sportsman's Club for Trap Shooting.

1. Traps, Kise And Bounds.|All matches shall be shot from H and T ground-traps, the choice of which the referee shall decide by toss.

The boundaries shall be eighty yards for single birds, and one hundred yards for double birds; which, in single-bird shooting, shall be measured from a point equidistant from, and in a directline between the two traps; in double-bird shooting, from a point equidistant from, and in direct line between, the centre traps.

2. Placing The Traps.|In single-bird shooting the distance between the traps shall be four yards ; in double-bird shooting, as four traps are used, the H and T traps shall be set alternately, and two yards apart.

3. Scoring.|After the party is at the score and ready to shoot, he shall take the bird or birds, unless barred by the referee.

The party at the score must not leave it to shoot, and must hold the butt of his gun below his elbow until the bird or birds rise ; and in case of infraction of this provision, the bird or birds shall be scored as missed.

4. Rising Of Birds.|All birds must be on the wing when shot at; all contingencies of misfire, non-explosion of cap, gun not cocked, etc., etc., are at the risk of the party shooting.

5. Recovering Birds.|It shall be optional with the party shooting to recover his own birds, or appoint a person for that purpose.

In all cases the birds shall be gathered by hand, without the use of extraneous means, within three minutes from the time it alights, or bescored a miss. A bird once out of bounds shall be scored a miss.

6. Loading.|The charge of shot shall not exceed one ounce and a half. All guns shall be loaded from the same charger, except in case of breech-loaders, when the referee may open one or more cartridges to ascertain if the charge of shot is correct. Any party infringing this rule shall lose the match.

7. Ties.|In case of a tie at single birds, the distance shall be increased five yards, and shall be shot off at five birds each. In case of a second tie, the distance shall be again increased five yards, tnd this distance shall be maintained till the match is decided. The ties in double-bird shooting shall be shot off at twenty-one yards, without any increase, at five double rises.

8. Judges And Referee.|Two judges and a referee shall be appointed before the shooting commences. The referee's decision shall be final. He shall have power to call " No bird," in case any birds fail to fly, and may allow a contestant another bird, in case the latter shall have been balked or interfered with, or may for any reason satisfactory to the referee be entitled to it.

In case of any unnecessary delay on the partof either of the contestants, the referee shall order the party so delaying to the score, and, in case of his failing to comply within five minutes, said party shall lose the match.

If a bird should fly towards parties within the bounds, in such a manner that to shoot at it would endanger any person, another bird will be allowed; and if a bird is shot at by any person besides the party at the score, the referee shall decide how it shall be scored, or whether a new bird shall be allowed.

Rules governing the Badge held by the Champion
Pig eon-Shooter of America.

We, the undersigned, contestants for the Badge of the Championship of America, given by Captain A. H. Bogardus, do hereby pledge ourselves and agree to the following rules and regulations, whenever and wherever said badge is contested for:

1. The winner of the badge shall give a satisfactory guarantee to Captain A. H. Bogardus for the safety thereof, in the shape of a responsible surety.

2. The winner shall pledge himself to shoot
any challenger, for a sum not less than $250 a side, within two months of the date of said challenge, under penalty of forfeiting said badge.

3. Any party challenging the holder of this badge shall make a deposit of $125, as a forfeit for a match of $250 a side, in the hands of the editor of the *Spirit of the Times,* to be covered by the challenged party with an equal amount. The balance of the money, $125 a side, shall be deposited in the hands of the editor of the *Spirit of the Times,* or some other party, mutually agreed upon by both parties, three days before the match is shot; the match then becomes play or pay. In case of the holder not complying with the foregoing conditions, he shall forfeit the badge to the party challenging.

4. Every contestant for this badge shall pledge himself to contend for the same under the rules of the Prairie Shooting Club of Chicago, with the exception that the single birds must be shot from ground-traps.

5. All matches for this badge shall be at one hundred pigeons, fifty single and twenty-five double rises, from H and T traps I the single from ground-traps and the double from plunge-traps.

6. The holder of this badge shall name theplace where the same shall be contested for, and each contestant shall furnish one hundred and ten pigeons for the match, and the pigeons shall be taken out of the same basket or box until the same is exhausted, and so on through the match.

7. Having tossed for first shot and trap, the second party shooting shall take the bird or birds in the remaining trap or traps, and so on through the match.

8. The party holding this badge for two years against all comers, it shall become his personal property.

Entries for the badge will be $50, and the winner of the badge to receive half the money, and the other half to go to the second best. The first match to take place the 20th day of March, 1874. -

The National Champion Badge.

Donated by Louis L. Lorillard, Esq., and Instituted by the " Spirit of the Times."

The holder of this badge shall leave a responsible security in the office of Wilkes's *Spirit of the Times,* for the forthcoming of the same whenever called for.

He shall shoot as often as once in three months, if challenged, for not less than $500 a side |that is to say, in one week from the time of the decision of any match the winner of the badge may be challenged again|and he shall shoot within three months from the date of the challenge. He shall have the naming of the place and time of shooting, subject to the approval of the editor of the *Spirit of the Times.*

In all cases he shall cover the money of the challenging party within one month, and name time and place of shooting, or, in failing to do so, shall forfeit the badge to the party challenging. Any party holding the badge for two years, it shall become his personal property.

Any party challenging for this badge shall deposit $250 in the hands of the editor of the *Spirit of the Times* as one-half forfeit. All the money from both parties to be up in said office one week previous to date of shooting, when the match becomes play or pay. Either party may compel the other to go to the score not later than one o'clock P.m.

The matches for this badge shall be shot according to the English rules, as modified and published below, at fifty single birds each, each party to bring not less than seventy birds on the ground.

Either party may trap and handle his quota of birds, or furnish a substitute.

The party commencing to trap shall continue until the match is half out, that is to say, until twenty-five birds each have been shot at, when the opposite party shall commence and trap an equal number. It shall be decided by " toss" which party commences trapping.

The referee, in all cases, unless amicably and mutually agreed upon, to be appointed by the editor of the *Spirit of the Times.*

In case of a tie, the parties shall shoot at five birds each; in case of a second, they shall shoot at five more, and so on until the match is decided, the condition covering trapping to apply the same as in the match.

Mules of the National Championship Badge.

Rule 1. The gun must not be carried to the shoulder until the bird is on the wing.

Rule 2. A misfire shall be at the risk of the shooter.

Rule 3. if a person pulls the trap without notice from the shooter, he has the option to take the bird or not.

Rule 4. If on the trap being pulled the bird does not rise, it is at the option of the shooter to take it or not; but if not, he must declare it by saying "No bird."

Rule 5. Each bird must be recovered within the boundary, eighty yards, within three minutes, if required by any party interested, or it must be scored lost. If a bird is challenged to show shot-mark, it must be handed to the referee for his decision.

Rule 6. If a bird that has been shot perches or settles on the top of the fence or on any of the buildings higher than the fence, it is to be scored a lost bird.

Rule 7. Or if a bird perches or settles on the top of a fence, or on any of the buildings higher than the fence, and then falls dead to the ground, it is a lost bird.

Rule 8. If a bird once out of the grounds should return and fall dead within the boundary, it must be scored a lost bird.

Rule 9. If the shooter advances to the trap and orders it to be pulled, and does not shootat the bird, or his gun is not properly loaded, or does not go off, the bird is to be scored lost.

Rule 10. Should a bird that has been shot be flying away, and a "scout" fires and brings the bird down within the boundary, the referee may, if satisfied the bird would not have fallen by the gun of the shooter, order it to be scored a lost bird; or, if satisfied the bird would have fallen, may order it to be scored a dead bird; or, if in doubt on the subject, he may order the shooter to shoot at another bird.

Rule 11. A bird shot on the ground with the first barrel is " no bird "; but it may be shot on the ground with second barrel if it has been fired at with the first barrel while on the wing.

Rule 12. The shooter is bound at any time to gather his bird, or depute some person to do so, when called on by his opponent; but in so doing he must not be assisted by any other person, or use any description of implement. Should the shooter be any way baffled by his opponent, or by any of the party shooting, he can claim another bird, with the sanction of the referee.

Rule 13. Shooting shall be from five traps.If more than one trap is pulled, so that more than one bird is on the wing or at large at the same time, the shooter has the option of shooting or not; if he kills, the bird must be scored; but should he miss, it shall be a lost bird.

Rule 14. The shooter cannot leave the shooting-mark under any pretence to follow up any bird that will not rise, but is walking away from the trap after it is pulled; and, having once left the mark after shooting at the bird, cannot return to shoot at it again under any circumstances. The amount of shot for each barrel shall not exceed one ounce and a quarter. Any shooter found to have a larger quantity in his gun, or who discharges his gun after his load is" challenged, shall be at once disqualified. The five ground traps shall be placed five yards apart, under the direction of the referee, thirty yards rise, and the use of both barrels is allowed.

Rule 15. Each shooter shall pull the traps for his opponent, or shall nominate a man to do so. The puller shall in all cases pull fairly, and without delay; and if the referee shall be satisfied that the trap was not pulled fairly, and without resort to any kind of baffling device, he shallorder the bird to be scored for the shooter, though not killed within bounds. The trap to be pulled to be decided by tossing a die by the referee, or by such other means as shall be just and satisfactory.

Rule 16. Each shooter shall come to the score on being called by the referee, and each may claim an intermission of fifteen minutes once during the match.

Rule 17. The boundary shall be measured from the centre of the middle trap.
Hides of the Prairie Shooting Club of Chicago.
[As Amended March 10, 1874.]

Rule 1. *Traps, Rise and Boundaries.* | All matches shall be shot from H and T plunge or lever traps, the choice of which the referee shall decide by toss. The boundaries shall be eighty yards for single birds, and one hundred yards for double birds, which shall be measured from a point equidistant from, and in a direct line between, the two traps, or, when more than two traps are used, in a direct line between the centre traps. The rise for single birds shall be twenty, one yards, and for double birds eighteen yards.

Rule 2. *Distance between Traps.*|In single- bird shooting, the distance between the traps shall be five yards; in double-bird shooting, when four traps are used, they shall be two and a half yards apart.

Rule 3. *Judges and Referee.*|Two judges and a referee shall be appointed before the shooting commences, and the referee's decision shall be final. He may allow a contestant another bird in case the latter shall have been balked or interfered with, if he thinks the party entitled to it.

Rule 4. *Birds and Decision.*|If a bird shall fly towards parties within the bounds, in such a manner that to shoot at it would endanger any person, another bird shall be allowed; and, if a bird is shot at within the bounds by any person besides the party at the score, the referee shall decide how it shall be scored, or whether another bird shall be allowed.

Rule 5. *Position at the Score.*|After the shooter has taken his stand at the score, he shall not level his gun or raise the butt above his elbow until the bird is on the wing. Should he infringe on this rule, the bird or birds shall be scored as lost, whether killed or not.

Rule 6. *Release of Birds.*|The shooter, whenready, to say " pull," and the puller to obey such signal, and pull the trap or traps fairly and evenly, and release the bird or birds instanter. If the trap be pulled or the birds released before the signal is given by the shooter, he shall have the option of calling " No bird" and refusing to shoot; but if he shoots, the bird shall be deemed a fair one, and scored for or against him, as the case may be.

Rule 7. *Rise and Catt of Birds.*|All birds must be on the wing when shot at, or will be scored as lost birds. If the bird does not rise immediately after the trap is pulled, the shooter shall have the option of calling " No bird "; and if he shoots at it on its afterward rising, it will . be considered " a lost bird."

Rule 8. *Gathering Birds.*|It shall be optional with the party shooting to gather his own birds or appoint a person to do so for him. In all cases the bird must be gathered by hand, without any forcible means, within three minutes from the time it alights, or be scored as lost. All " birds" must show shot-marks if challenged. A bird once out of bounds shall be scored as lost.

Rule 9. *Misfires.* | Should a gun miss fire or fail to discharge from any cause, it shall scoreas a lost bird, unless the referee finds, upon examination, that the gun was properly loaded, and the misfire unavoidable, in which case he shall allow another bird.

Rule 10. *Birds on the Wing.* | In double shooting, both birds must be on the wing when the first is shot at. If but one bird flies, and one barrel is fired or snapped, the birds shall not be scored, whether killed or missed, but the party shooting shall have two more birds; or, if both birds fly and are killed with one barrel, he must shoot at two other birds.

Rule 11. *Size of Gun.*|The shooter shall not .be allowed to use a gun of larger calibre than that known as No. 10.

Rule 12. *Charge of Shot.*|There shall be no restriction as to size of shot used or charge of powder, but the charge of shot shall be not to exceed the regular Dixon Measure, No. 1106 or No. 1107, 1 oz. by measure struck off.

Rule 13. *Penalty for Overloading.*|The Club shall provide a standard shot measure, and all guns shall be loaded from the same, except in case of breech-loaders, when the referee may open one or more cartridges, to ascertain if the charge of shot is not above the standard. Any person found infringing on this rule shall be barred from further participation in the match.

Rule 14. *Ties and Distances.*|In ease of ties at single birds, the distance shall be increased five yards. In case of second tie, the distance shall be increased five yards further, and this distance shall be maintained until the match is decided, and shall be shot off at five single birds. The ties on double-bird shooting shall be shot off at twenty-one yards at five double rises.

Rule 15. *Ties.*|At a shooting match, all ties shall be shot off on the same grounds immediately after the match, if they can be concluded before sunset. In case they cannot be concluded by sunset, they shall be concluded on the following day, unless otherwise directed by the judges or referee. This, however, shall not prevent the ties from dividing the prizes, if they may all agree to do so. Should one refuse to divide, then it must be shot off. Any one of the ties being absent thirty minutes after the time agreed upon to shoot them off shall forfeit his right to contest for the prize.

Rule 16. *Bribing and Penalty.* | Any competitor or other person bribing, or attempting to bribe, the trapper or puller, or attempting to obtain an unfair advantage in any manner whatsoever, to be disqualified from shooting or sharing in the results of the match.

Rule 17. *To prevent Accidents.*|The shooter, if he use a breech-loader, shall not put the cartridge in his gun until called to the score. If he use a muzzle-loader, he shall leave it uncapped until called.

Rule 18. *Challenging and Penalties.* | Any person participating in a match shall have the privilege of challenging a competitor as to charge of shot used, and the referee shall make such challenged party draw his charges and have them examined ; and, if found to exceed the limit fixed by rule, he shall forfeit his right to participate in the match, or share in the same in any way. If he fires his gun after being challenged, and before the charge has been examined by the referee, he shall suffer the same penalty as for overloading.

Rule 19. *Time at Score.*|Each participant in a shooting match shall hold himself in readiness, and come to the score prepared to shoot when his name is called by the scorer. If he be longer than five minutes, it shall be discretionary with the referee whether to allow him to shoot or not in the match.

13 FANEUIL HALL SQUARE, BOSTON, .jfeSr&w MASS.
Importers of & Dealers in
Breech and Muzzle-Loading Guns.
W. C. Scott & Son's, Westley Richard's, Greener's, Webley's, Moore's
and others.
Also, Remington's, Whitney's, and other American makes.

Maynard's, BaUard's, Remington's, Steven's, and other Sporting Rifles. Agents for W. C. SCOTT & SON'S BKEECH LOADERS.

Every size of these celebrated Breech-Loading Guns constantly in stockl14, 12,10, 8, and 4 boreslor imported to special order, if desired. Scott's Illustrated Book on Breech-Loaders, bound in morocco, 25 cts. by mail.

Bussey's Patent Gyro-Pigeon Trap for Shooting Practice.

AUo, Fine Trout and Salmon Rods, Flies, Reels, and every article in Fishing Tackle. Send For Circulars.

JOSEPH BUTLER & CO.,
179 E. MADISON STREET, CHICAGO,

Winners of the Chicago Gun Trial of 1874, *at Dexter Park, wider the auspices of tJtt Illinois State Sportsmen's Association.*

Messrs. BTTTLER & CO. respectfully invite the attention of the Sportsmen to the report of the Gun Trial, from which It will be seen that g-uns of their own manufacture, and those rebored by them, excelled both in pattern and penetration those of any other maker.

Messrs. BUTLER & CO. make a specialty of reboring guns to shoot properly, and that the enviable reputation they have achieved for this class of work is deserved, the following extracts from the above report clearly prove:

" Three highest averages for Pattern, Daniel T. Elston, owner,|101, 1-6. Rebored by J. Butler & Co. Manufactured by J. Buti.ir & Co., owners,| 181, 3-6. Manufactured by]. Butler $ Co., owners,lltd, t-6."

Breech-Loaders of their own manufacture are warranted unexcelled by those of any other maker.

Bach and every part of the *gun* is carefully examined by Mr. BUTLER before leaving the store. Kepairins of all kinds neatly done. We keep in stock every quality of W. C. Scott & Son's Breech-Loaders. winners of the Gun Trial of 1873, In New York. W. W. Greener's and other celebrated makers kept in stock. Gun materlnl of all kinds. Powder, Shot, and Caps, Ely's Ammunition and Metalic Co.'s Shells and Caps, Berdan Shells, and Draper & Co.'s Shells, &c., &c. A full stock of J. B. McHarg & Co.'s and Bradford & Anthony's Fishing Tackle, consisting of Bamboo Rods, Bass and Trout Rods. Reels, Spoon Bait, Plies, Silkworm Gut, Plated Linen and Silk Lines, Gut and Gimp Fish Hooks, and everything in the ling. Sportsmen visiting the West will find every requisite for a complete outfit. Parties from the Eitst can have Shells loaded to order on short notice, and shipped to any parts of the States, A full stock kept constantly on Hand. Ground and Plunge Traps.

TO SPORTS ME 1ST
DROP SHOT.

*Compared with any other, will
be found Cleaner, Heavier,
and more Uniform,*
A WEEKLY JOURNAL (OF SIXTEEN PAGES),
DEVOTED TO
FIELD SPOET8,
Fish Culture, Protection of Game, Preservation of Forests,
YACHTING, BOATING,
AND ALL
OUT-DOOR RECREATION & STUDY.
IT IS THE OFFICIAL OEGAN OF THE
AMERICAN FISH CULTURISTS' ASSOCIATION,
JfOtjesf attfr
Is the only Journal published In this country that fully supplies the wants and meets the necessities of the
Gentleman 'Sportsman.
SEND FOB SPECIXEN COPT. TERM8, $B A YEAR.
Address:
Forest and Stream Publishing Company,
17 CHATHAM ST. (City Hall Square), NEW YOEK. 125 SOUTH THIRD ST., PHILADELPHIA. 124 DEARBORN ST., CHICAGO.

-the SPORTMAN's Oracle & Country
GENTLEMAN'S NEWSPAPER,
A Weekly Review and Chronicle of the
Turf, Field and Aquatic Sports,
AGRICULTURE, ART, SCIENCE,
LITERATURE, CHESS, DRAUGHTS, BILLIARDS, VETERINARY, SHOOTING, FISHING,
ff, Athletic Pastimes, Natural History,
anb *it* grants.

rpHE TURF, FIELD AND FARM, having by far the largest circular J- tion of any paper of its class published in the country, is, by its culture and ability, the recognized authority on all the subjects of which it treats, as its high moral tone and advocacy of healthy, elevating and manly sports have won for it the approval and active patronage of the best and most intelligent people in the land ; and the substantial evidence of its growing popularity is the continual and steady increase of circulation through 3ut the WORLD.

Every Turf Association, Agricultural Society, Horse Owner, Stock Breeder, Club and Library, should subscribe and have on file, for reference, a journal representing the vast interests advocated by the TURF, FIELD AND FARM.

TO THOSE WHO ADVERTISE.

The TURF, FIELD AND FARM has an undisputed claim to be one of the best general advertising mediums in the United States. Its circulation throughout the world has increased three fold during the past three years without increase of rates, and is still extensively spreading. The paper is read by tens of thousands every week, while

Horsemen, Sportsmen, Farmers, and the lovers of aquatic and kindred sports preserve and bind their copies.

Specimen copies, with premium lists, catalogue of publications, etc., Bent upon application.

TURF, FIELD AND FARM ASSOCIATION,
Office: 3i Park .Row, New York.
For Sale by Newsdealers throughout the World.
BARTON, ALEXANDER, & WALLER,
1O1 and 103 Duane Street, New York,
IMPORTERS AND DEALERS IN
Breech and Muzzle-Loading Guns
OF ALL THE BEST MAKERS.
KIFLES, PISTOLS, AMMUNITION,
And Sportsmens Goods *of all Kinds.*
FISHING TACKLE
OF EVERY VAEIETY.
FISH HOOKS, RODS, REELS, LINES, &c.
Artificial Flies and Baits on band and made to order.
FINEST QUALITY SPLIT BAMBOO FLY RODS
FOR TEOXJT AND SALMON FISHING.
s for tlie
UNITED STATES ARMS CO.'S REVOLVERS.
Alexander's Pocket Cutlery. JOHN W. COUKT & CO.'S FISH HOOKS.THE tmes:

THE AMERICAN GENTLEMAN'S NEWSPAPER,
Annual Subscription, $5.00.
WEEKLY,
IN HANDSOME FOHM.

rpHIS Journal is devoted to Field Sports, Accounts of Ex- -L ploration and adventure, Exploits on Flood and Field and in the Jungle and the Forest, the Current History and Philosophy of the Turf, the Science of Breeding and Raising Running and Trotting Horses, Yachting, including the science of construction, Hunting, Fishing, Billiards, the Stage, and the Literature of the day. An especial feature is

THE VETERINARY DEPARTMENT.

One of the most able and successful Veterinary Surgeons of the age answers questions and gives directions and prescriptions, *gratis,* for the relief and cure of Horses, Cattle, Dogs, etc., suffering from disease or injury by accident. Hundreds of subscribers declare this department to be Wobth The Whole Subscription.

THE SPIRIT OF THE TIMES

Also gives carefully considered answers, judicial in their nature and thoroughly impartial, to questions in dispute among gentlemen, and submitted by the parties for authoritative decision. It also resolves questions of interest where no dispute exists and no money is involved, but where information is desired. The readers value these columns of The Spibit very highly.

OUR CORPS OF CORRESPONDENTS is unrivaled.

GEORGE WILKES,
Editor and Proprietor,
3 Park Sow, If. Y.
mmrait
CONTAINS AT.T. THE
LATEST RIFLE NEWS;
FULL SCORES OF SHOOTING
Practical Natural History ;
Fishing and Gunning.
Price, 1O Cents.
SGH1IYLER, HAETLEY & GRAIAI,
IMPORTERS AND MANUFACTURERS OF
GUNS, RIFLES, PISTOLS
SPORTING ARTICLES,
19 Maiden Lane, 2O & 22 John St., yew York.
BREECH-LOADING GUNS A SPECIALTY.

Fine Guns and Rifles manufactured and imported to order. Agents for the Union Metallic Cartridge Company.

The Slurtevant Brass Shell for Breech-Loading Shot Guns.
4PW BLACK'S |7 I PATENT
fifflttrfljp? CARTRIDGE *mm* VEST.

This vest affords the best arrangement for carrying cartridges yet Invented. The weight is so evenly distributed that it is scarcely felt. The heads of the cartridges can be carried down, which is of importance when the brass shells are used, as in carrying them with the heads up the weight of the shot of ten forces the wad forward, when bad shooting is the result. The vest is made of English fustian, and is a sportsmanlike garment.

Price, each $7.SO.
In ordering send measurement around the chest, and gauge of gun.
SCHUYLER, HARTLEY & GRAHAM,
19 Maiden. Lane, New York.
Send for Circular.
Stnrtevant's Patent Brags Shell for BreecL - Loading |.| Sinn Gang.
Works Published by J. B. Ford & Co.
THE CIRCUIT RIDER.
A Novel.
By EDWARD EGGLESTON.
Author of " The Hoosier Schoolmaster" etc., etc.

I vol. I2mo. Illustrated. Cloth, $i.75.

"The breezy freshness of the Western prairie blended with the refinements ol literary culture. It is alive with the sound of rushing streams and the echoes ol the forest, but shows a certain graceful self-possession which betrays the presence of ihe artist's power."|JV. K. *Tribune.*
A GOOD MATCH.

A Novel.
By AMELIA PERKIER, Author of "Mea Culpa."

I vol. I2mo. Cloth, $i.50.
A clever and amusing Novel, agreeably written, racy, and lively.

u A very readable love story, tenderly I " The characters appear and act with told.'|*Hearth and Home.* a real life."|*Providence Press*
BRAVE HEARTS.
A Novel.
By ROBERTSON GRAY.
I vol. I2mo. Illustrated. Cloth, $i.75.

A characteristic American tale, with Illustrations by Darley, Stephens, Frank Beard, and Kendrick.
" About as pure, breezy, and withal, I " Its pictures of the strange life of readable, a story of American life as we I those early Californian days are simply have met with this long time."|*Con-* j admirable, quite as good as anything *gregationatist.* Bret Harte has written."|*Lit, World.*
SILVER AND GOLD.
AN ACCOUNT OF THE MINING AND METALLURGICAL INDUSTRY OF THE UNITED STATES, WITH REFERENCE CHIEFLY TO THE PRECIOUS METALS.
By ROSSITER W. RAYMOND.
U.S. Commissioner Mining Statistics; Pres't. Am. Inst. Mining Engineers ; Editor Engineering and Mining Journal; Author of " Mines, Mills, and Furnaces," etc., etc. I vol. 8vo. Cloth, $3.50.
"Valuable and exhaustive work on a o the world of
theme of great import t industry.' |*Pkiladelphi
a Inquirer.*
" A repository of much valuable current information."|*N.Y, Tribune.*
27 *Park Plact, and* 24 cr 26 *Murray Street, New York.*PRINCIPLES OF DOMESTIC SCIENCE
AS APPLIED TO THE DUTIES AND PLEASURES OF HOME.
By CATHARINE E. BEECHER and HARRIET BEECHER STOWE
I vol. I2mo. *Profusely Illustrated.* Cloth, $2.
Prepared with a view to assist in training young women for the distinctive duties which inevitably come upon them in household life, this volume has been made with especial reference to the duties, cares, and pleasures of *the family,* as being the place where, whatever the political developments of the future, woman, from her nature of body and of spirit, will find her most engrossing occupation. It is full of interest for all intelligent girls and young women.
The work has been heartily indorsed and adopted by the directors of many of the leading Colleges and Seminaries for young women as a text-book, both for study and reading.

MINES, MILLS, AND FURNACES of the Precious Metals of the United States. BEING A COMPLETE EXPOSITION OF THE GENERAL METHODS EMPLOYED IN THE GREAT MINING INDUSTRIES OF AMERICA.
By ROSSITER W. RAYMOND, Ph. D.,
U. S. Commissioner of Mining Statistics.
I vol. 8vo. *With Plates.* Cloth, $3 50.

This is a very particular account of the condition of the mining interests, and the processes and mechanical appliances which are applicable to them, in California, Nevada, Oregon, Idaho, Montana, Utah, Arizona, Wyoming, Colorado, and New Mexico. It is the report of the Commissioner to the Secretary of the Treasury, and embodies all the information which official investigation and contributions from experts and residents of those regions can afford.

" The author is thorough in his subject, and has already published a work on our mines which commanded universal approval by its clearness of statement and breadth of views,"|*Albany Argus.*

His scientific ability, his practical
knowledge of mines and mining, his unerring judgment, and, finally, the enthusiasm with which he enters upon his work, all combine to fit him for his position, and none could bring it to a greater degree of uprightness and fairness.1 '|*Denver News.*

J3T Any of the above books will be soul to any address, post-paid, upon receipt of the price by tlie Publishers.
27 *Park Pla:e, and* 24 6 26 *Murray Street, New York.*
W"*orks Published by /. B. Ford cf Co.*

NEW LIFE IN NEW LANDS.

NOTES OF TRAVEL ACROSS THE AMERICAN CONTINENT, FROM CHICAGO TO THE PACIFIC AND BACK.

BY GRACE GREENWOOD.
I vol. I2mo. $2.

This is a gathered series of letters, racy, brilliant, piquant; full of keen observation and pungent statement of facts, picturesque in delineation of scenes on the plains, in the mountains, and along the sea.

"Among the best of the author's productions, and every way delightful." |*Boston Post.*

" The late William H. Seward characterized her account of Mormons and Mormonism as the most graphic and trustworthy he had ever read. |*Methodist Home Journal.*

" Grace always finds lots of things no one else would see ; and she has a happy knack of picking up the mountains ana cities and big tress, and tossing them across the continent right before the reader's eyes. It's very convenient."| *Buffalo Express,*

MY WIFE AND I:
OR, HARRY HENDERSON'S
A Novel.

HISTORY.
By HARRIET BEECHER STOWE.
Illustrated. I vol. I2mo. Cloth, $i 75.

This charming novel is, in some respects, Mrs. Stowe's most thoughtful and complete book. It is eminently a book for the times, giving the author's individual ideas about the much-vexed *Woman Question* including marriage, divorce, suffrage, legislation, and all the rights claimed by the clamorous.

" A capital story, in which fashionable follies are shown up, fast young ladies weighed in the balance and found wanting, nnd the value of true worth exited."|*Portland A rgus.*

bioite

"Always bright, piquant, and entertaining, with" an occasional touch of tenderness, strong because subtle, keen in sarcasm, full of womanly logic directed against unwomanly tendencies. |*Boston Journal.*

THE OVERTURE OF ANGELS.
A SERIES OF PICTURES OF THE ANGELIC APPEARANCES ATTENDING
THE NATIVITY OF OUR LORD. A CHAPTER FROM
THE "LIFE OF CHRIST."
By HENRY WARD BEECHER.
Illustrated. I vol. I2mo. $2.

A beautiful and characteristically interesting treatment of all the events recorded in the Gospels as occurring about the time of the Nativity. Full of poetic imagery, beauty of sentiment, and vivid pictures of the life of the Orient in that day.

u The style, the sentiment, and faith- I commend it to many readers) to whom fulness to the spirit of the Biblical record j its elegance of form will giv: H an aiidi-
with which the narrative is treated are characteristic of its author, and will
tional attraction."|*Worcater (Mass.*
Sty.
" A perfect fragment."- .*V. Y. World.*
7 *Park Place, and* 24 &' 26 *Murray Street, New York,*

THE CHILDREN'S WEEK:
SEVEN STORIES FOR SEVEN DAYS.
By R. W. RAYMOND. Illustrated By H. L. Stephens And Miss M. L. Hallock.
i vol. l6mo. Cloth, $l 25.

Seven cheery stories with a flavor of the holidays about them. Mr. Raymond's conceptions are ingenious, and while the glimpses of fairy-land and its wonders will open the eyes of the little folk, the book possesses many attractions for older persons in its simple, artistic style, and the quaint ideas in which it revels.

" The book is bright enough to please any people of culture, and yet so simple th:it children will welcome it with glee." |*Cleveland Plaindealer.*

Mr. Raymond's tales have won great popularity by their wit, delicate fancy,
and, withal, admirable good sense. The illustrations|all new and made for the book|are particularly apt and pleasing, showing forth the comical element of the book and its pure and beautiful sentiment."|*Buffalo (N. Y.) Commercial A dvertiser.*

OUR SEVEN CHURCHES:

EIGHT LECTURES.
By THOMAS K. BEECHER.
I vol. i6mo. Paper, 50 cents ; Cloth, $i.

A most valuable exponent of the doctrines of the leading religious denominations, and a striking exhibition of the author's magnanimity and breadth of loving sympathy.
u The sermons are written in a style at once brilliant, epigrammatic, and readable."|*Utica Herald.*
" This little book has created considerable discussion among the religious journals, and will be read with interest by all."|*Phila. Ledger.*
"There is hardly a page which does not offer a fresh thought, a genial touch of humor, or a suggestion at which the reader's heart leaps up with grateful surprise that a minister belonging to a sect can think and speak so generously and nobly."|*Milwaukee Sentinel.*

HISTORY of the STATE OF NEW YORK.
FROM THE DATE OF THE DISCOVERY AND SETTLEMENTS ON MANHATTAN ISLAND TO THE PRESENT TIME. A TEXT-BOOK FOR HIGH SCHOOLS, ACADEMIES, AND COLLEGES.
By S. S. RANDALL,
Superintendent of Public Education in New York City.
I vol. I2mo. *Illustrated.* Cloth, $i 75.

Officially adopted by the Boards of Education in the cities of New York, Brooklyn, and Jersey City, for use in the Public Schools ; and in Private Schools throughout the State.

27 *Park Place, and* 24 *&* 26 *Murray Street, New York.Works Published by J. B. Ford & Co.*

LECTURES TO YOUNG MEN
ON VARIOUS IMPORTANT SUBJECTS.

NEW EDITION, WITH ADDITIONAL LECTURES,
By HENRY WARD BEECHER.
Uniform Edition of the Author's Works.
I vol. I2mo. Cloth, $i 50.

This was Mr. Beecher's first book, and is known all over the world. The present edition is enriched by the addition of several new lectures, and some reminiscences of the origin of the book by Mr. Beecher. The book should have a place in every family. It can scarcely fail to interest every intelligent reader, nor to benefit every young man who reads it.
' The subjects are all practical, and presented with characteristic impress- iveness."|A *Ibany Evening Journal.*
u Wise and elevating in tune, pervaded by earnestness, and well fitted for its missi of th. . . ..
" These lectures are written with all the vigor of style and beauty of lan
ion to improve and benefit the youth e land."-|*Boston Commonwealth.*

guage which characterize everything from the pen of this remarkable man They are a series of fearless dissertations upon every-day subjects, conveyed with a power of eloquence and a practical illustration so unique as to be oftentimes startling to the reader of ordinary discourses of the kind."| *Philadelphia Inquirer.*

MOTHERLY TALKS
WITH YOUNG HOUSEKEEPERS.

By MRS. H. W. BEECHER.
WITH CARBON-PHOTOGRAPHIC PORTRAIT OF THE AUTHOR.
I vol. I2mo. $2.

Mrs. Beecher's notion of woman's sphere is, that, whatever exceptional women may be able to accomplish by reason of peculiar circumstances and talents, the place of labor and achievement for most women, and for all married women and mothers, is *Hcmt.*

This- book, composed of brief and pithy articles on almost every conceivable point of duty, is an admirable monitor for young wives, and a mine of good sense and information for growing maidens.

" An admirable correctre to ignorance in the household."|AT. *Y. Triiune.*

u A useful and entertaining work, Crammed with friendly and admirable monitions and instruction for young housekeepers." | *1'hiladclpHia Evening Herald.*

n This book is exactly what its title Bets forth|a kind and motherly way of helping the young and inexperienced
make agreeable, well-regulated, and happy homes."|*Boston Globe,*

"What she has to say she says M well, with such good sense, ripe judgment, and such a mother-warmth of heart, that she cannot fail to help the class for whom she writes, and guid them into good and useful paths."| *Presbyterian.*

3j Park Place, and 24 *&* 26 *Murray Street. New York.*WINNING SOULS.

4KKTCHKS AND INCIDENTS DURING FORTY YEARS OF PASTORAL WORK

By REV. S. B. HALLIDAY.
I vol. izmo. Cloth, $i.

The author of this volume for some time past has been, and now is, engaged as assistant in the pastoral labors of Plymouth Church, Brooklyn (Rev. H. W. Beecher's), where, in visiting among the sick, the poor, and the afflicted of that large parish, he is continually encountering new and interesting phases of heart-life. These simple records of scenes among his earlier labors possess a peculiar interest.

" Full of valuable suggestions to ministers in the department of active duty." |*Methodist Recorder.*

" The book is tenderly written, and
many of its pathetic scenes will be read with moistened eyes. We commend the book to pastors and people."|*Boston Christian Era.*

NORWOOD:
Or, Village Life in New England.

A Novel.

By HENRY WARD BEECHER.
Uniform Edition of the Author's Work

I vol. izmo. Illustrated. *[In Pntr,*
This is Mr. Beecher's only novel, and it affords a most remarkable illustration of his versatility. Full of exquisite descriptions of scenery and delineations of social and domestic life, exceedingly graphic and trustworthy in detail, and abounding in passages of genial humor and kindly wisdom, it is altogether one of the most enjoyable novels ever published. It is fragrant with the genuine raciness of the New England soiL

PLEASANT TALK ABOUT FRUITS, FLOWERS, AND FARMING.
MEW EDITION, WITH MUCH ADDITIONAL MATTES,
By HENRY WARD BEECHER.
Uniform Edition of the Author's Works.
I vol. I2mo. Cloth, $2. oo.

This volume, when it was first given to the public some years ago, was most favorably received, both in this country and in England. The present edition contains many recent additions to the original book, dealing with both the poetical and the practical side of gardening and fanning, the whole making a volume of rare interest and value.

27 *Park Place, and* 24 6 26 *Murray Street, New York.*
THE PIONEER GUN, Still Aliead!!
EVERY FIRST PRIZE FOR TRAP SHOOTING
At the last convention of the
KEW YORK STATE ASSOCIATION

WON WITH "THE PAKZER"!
Messrs. Newell And Hambi/eton, winners of the only prize given for " making the largest score in the three regular shoots,"
Both Shot The Parker Onii!!
Two of the three winners of the Grand State Prize,
"the Dean Richmond Cup,"

THE PARKER GKLOST!!-&J
Medal and Diplomag awarded THE PARKER ULX,
When placed on exhibition in
COMPETITION OPEN TO THE WORLD.
MEDAL, AND DIPLOMA
From the American Institutel1869.
SILVER MEDAL
Texas State Fair, 1871.
SILVER MEDAL,
Texas State Fuir, 1873.
SILVER MEDAL

Mechanics and Agricultural Fair Association of Louisiana|1872.
DIPLOMA
From the Vermont Stato Agricultural Society|18ti8.

DIPLOMA
From the New Hampshire State Agricultural Society|18C8.

DIPLOMA
From the New Haven County (Conn.) Agricultural Society|1867.

DIPLOMA
From the Sardis (Mass.) Agricultural and Mechanical Society, 1870.

DIPLOMA
From the Connecticut Valley Agricultural Association|1870.

DIPLOMA
Agricultural and Mechanical Association of West Alabama|1871.

DIPL OMA
Adams County (Miss.) Agricultural and Mechanical Association|1872.

FIRST PREMIUM
At the Delaware County (Iowa) Fair|1871.

Send For Heduced Price List, Mat Ist, 1874.
Prices, $45, $50, $60, $65, $75, $80, $100, $105, $150, $200,$250.
Rclxninding-Loclis included.
PARKER BROTHERS, West Meriden, Conn.
SPORTING POWDER,
MANUFACTURED BY
LAFLIN & RAND POWDER COMPANY,
IS W YORK.
ORANGE LIGHTNING POWDER.
  This Is the strongest and cleanest powder made. Nos. 1 to 7. Packed only in sealed 1 Ib. canisters. The coarser sizes are especially recommended to owners of breech-loading guns, giving great penetration with very slight recoil. For trap shooting use No. 5 in guns of 12 gauge, and No. 6 in those of 10 gauge.
  ORANGE DUCKING POWDER.
  A very strong, clean powder, good for all shooting. Nos. 1 to 5. Especially adapted to killing clucks and geese at long range, and less liable to be aifected by dampness than other brands. Packed in 6% Ib. kegs, in 5 Ib. canisters, and 1 Ib. canisters.
  AUDI) BON.
  This is a very quick, clean powder for woodcock and quail shooting. Nos. 1 to 4. Packed in 12X ib- kegs, 6X Ib. kegs, and in 1 Ib. canisters.

ORANGE RIFLE POWDER.

This is more generally used for field shooting than any of the other brands, being less costly than the higher grades, and giving nearly the same results in the field.

No powder made of this grade will show such cleanliness as Orange Rifle. Packed in 25 Ib. kegs, ZX Ib. kegs, 6X Ib. kegs, and in 1 Ib. canisters. Sizes, P, FF, FFF.

All the above kinds of powder will give greater penetration and leave less residuum in the gun than any other brands known.

The LAFLIN AND RAND POWDER COMPANY are engaged in the manufacture of Gunpowder for sporting and also for mining purposes on the largest scale, having their factories at many different points. Sporting powder is, however, made by them only in the State of New York, taking its name from the old Orange Mills in Orange Co. Their mills have the most approved methods and perfect appointments, and the product is shipped to their magazines in all parts of the country, and to foreign ports. The reputation of the Orange Powder, established many years since, will be carefully guarded.

Branches of the house are established at St. Louis, Chlcapro, Du- buque, Buffalo, and Baltimore, besides agencies in all the principal towus aud cities.

USE THE

Double-Barreled, Breech-Load ing Shot Gun,

Whltmore's Patents, August 8, 1871. JLpril 16, 1873.

We are now prepared to furnish our Improved Double-barrelEd Breech-lo Ading Shot Gun, which we reco mmend as the best ever offered the American sportsman, combining all the most desirable features of the best English double guns, together with some valuable improvements not fouud in any other.

lu the prod uction of these guns no expense or trouble has been spared.

In order to suit the requirements of our d ifferent customers, we make three styles of gun, differing *onlii in the finish and kind of barrels and stocks,* which we offer at the full owing prices:

Plain VVnlnnt Slock. IV- carboiiizvtl Steel Bar- rels, - 845 UO

Fancy Stock, Twist Barrels, —— (ill ts)

Extra Finish Stock, Da- mascus or other Fancy Twist Barrels, En- graved Lock Plate, - - 75 00

In all of these guns only the best materials and workmanship are employed.

In order to enable us to offer a thoroughly well made and reliable gun at the low price of $45, we have ojiitted all ornamentation of either the stock or metal work, leaving both tip and butt stock plain.

Longth of barrel, 28. 30 inches. Bore, 10, 12 gauge. Weight: 28 inches, No. 12 gauge, *8% lbs.*: No. 10 sraugs, 8 lbs. 80 inches, No. 12 gaasfe, 8% lbs.; No. 10 gauge, *8% Ihi.*

t3P" In fixing upon the model of our 0-im, we have chosen what we think best adapted to meet the wants of the public. We cannot vary, in Any Particular, from the dimensions and weight before mentioned, or in the style of finish. Send for illustrated Catalogue and price-list. Address

MANTJFACTOKY: 1 LION, Herklmer Co., N. V.
REMINGTON & SONS,
281 and 283 Broadway, N. Y.
P. O. BOX, .-S994.
A JOURNAL FOR THE SPORTSMEN OF TO-DAY.
IGVERY S
179 EAST MADISON STREET, CHICAGO.
Terms Of Subscription : *Payable In advance. Yearly,* $4.00 ; *half yearly,* $2.00.
Forebjn and Canadian Subscription, post free | yearly, 18s. ; *half-yearly,* 9s.
Single copies, 10 *cents.*

nHE FIELD is a complete weekly review of the higher branches of . sport | Shooting, Fishing, Racing: and Trotting, Yachting and Rowing, Base Ball, Cricket, Billiards, and General Sporting News, Music and the Drama.

THE FIELD will be found in keeping with the times on all subjects pertaining to honorable sport, and will, under no circumstances, admit to its columns anything tending in anywise to demoralize or degrade public sentiment.

THE FIELD being the only Sporting Journal published west of New Tork, and the recognized authority among the sportsmen of the West and South, among whom it enjoys a large and increasing patronage, possesses superior advantages as an advertising medium, which will bo appreciated by those desiring to make their business known in tl.o United States.

Agents For Great Britain.| Messrs. Kirby & Endean, 190 Oxford Street, London.
KOTICE TO THE TRADE.
News Agents desirous of being supplied with THE FIELD are requested to apply to the publishers, 179 East Madison Street, from whom only it can be obtained.
F. J. .A.BBEY & CO.,
MANUFACTURERS AND IMPORTERS OF
Breech and Muzzle-Loading Guns
RIFLES AND PISTOLS.
Dealers in Fishing Tackle and General Sporting Goods.
Bad Shooting Guns made to shoot well.
SHELLS LOADED TO ORDER.
43 S. CLARK STREET, CHICAGO, Itt.
JOSEPH TOsTKS,
GUN MANUFACTURER,
45 & 49 Union St., and 1 Marshall St., Boston.
IMPORTER AND DEALER IN
GUNS, RIFLES, REVOLVERS & CUTLERY,

Parker Breech-Loading Shot-Gun.

Breech-Loading Shot-Guns of celebrated Ensllsh makers. Paper and Metallic Shells for Shot-Guns of all kinds. Metallic Cartridges for Rifles, Revolvers and Pistols. Caps, Wads, Powder, Shot, &e., &c. Pocket Cutlery, Razors, Scissors, &c. Alr-Guns and Cap Rifles for Saloons and Fairs. Fire Arms Repaired.

SPORTSMEN'S DEPOT.
JOHN KRIDER,
CORNER SECOND & WALNUT STREETS, PHILADELPHIA,
IMPORTER, MANUFACTURER AND DEALER *IS*
GUNS, RIFLES, PISTOLS
FISHING TACKLE OF ALL, KINDS.

He invites all Sportsmen and dealers in his line to examine his stock of Flies and Spliced Bamboo Rods, which are the best in this country. We make Flies of all kinds to order, or rods of any style.

Has constantly on hand a full assortment of Rods, Hooks, Lines, Baits, Reels, Hooks, Salmon Flies, Waterproof Silk Lines, Silk and Hair Trout Lines, &c. Perch Snoods, China and Grass Lines. Also, a large lot of Cane Reeds, Bamboo and Japan.

MANUFACTURER OF
FINE BREECH & MUZZLE-LOADING GUNS
TO ORDER.
A. Full Assortment of Sportsmen's Implements and Fishing Tackle.
No. 131 WALNUT STREET, PHILADELPHIA.
PIGEONJTRAPS.
"H" and "T"
PLUNGE TRAPS.
Common Traps . . . (per pair) $15.00
Patent Self-Closing Traps " 25.00

A pair of these Traps sent by freight or express on receipt of price.
W. F. PARKER,
Wc&t Meriden, Conn.
STANDARD,
. Patent Sifted Eagle Brand
CHILLED
DROP SHOT
AS ADOPTED BY THE
Net Yori State Ssortti's Association,
THOS. OTIS LE EOT & CO.,
PATENT SHOT &' LEAD WORKS,
261 & 263 WATER STREET,
NEW YOKK,
SOJLE MAISTUFACTUEERS.
84 & 86 CHAMBER STREET, NEW YORK,
MANUFACTURERS OF THB
CHARLES DALY

BEEECH-LOADING GTJNS.

These Guns ore pronounced by every dealer and sportsman who has handled them to be the finest finished and *closest* and *strongest shooting* Guns in the market. The barrels are of beautiful pattern and finish, and the locks and mountings of the best quality.

For sale by all the first-class Gun Dealers at our prices :
Side Snap Action $100.00 to $110.00
Top Snap Action, Double Bolt 130.00 " 175.00
Pistol Grip Stocks (extra) 10.00 |
Extra Close and Hard Shootinir guaranteed for 12.00 extra.
Agents for TTM. fOWEI.Ii & SONS.
WM, POWELL & SONS' BREECH-LOADERS

Have acquired, during the past few years, *the first place* in the estimation of English sportsmen; as they come into use in this country, they are coming to be known as *the best gun made in England.*
UNIVERSITY OF CALIFORNIA LIBRARY
BERKELEY

Return to desk from which borrowed.
This book is DUE on the last date stamped belc

APR 2'68-12 AM
LD 21-